Gianluigi Olivari

Unconscious sales techniques

Unleash your inner powerful sales techniques for outstanding sales success!

This page intentionally left blank

This page intentionally left blank

TABLE OF CONTENTS

1 - FOREWORD

This book was meant to provide an effective tool to those who are engaged in selling activities. The book is suitable for sales people of any age, experience and seniority (it works well for fresh appointed reps as well as experienced ones) and its suggestions can lead to sales excellence. Its background comes from the most recent findings on the functioning of the mind, combined with the experience gained by the author in many years of direct selling, in managing sales networks of various sizes, and in designing and delivering advanced sales training to Fortune 500 companies. The author has deliberately decided to make the text agile, fresh and of simple enjoyment, avoiding traditional sales techniques, assuming that readers are already well experienced in this regard.

The point of view of this book involves the exploration of usually almost completely neglected skills by traditional authors who write about sales. These skills, by the most open and advanced neurobiologists and psychologists, are believed to be responsible for 95% of the results that the individual is able to obtain in the course of his / her life.

These skills are mostly unconscious, and can be developed and utilized to enable any salesperson to achieve excellent sales results, without increasing the time and efforts (in many cases already extremely high) invested in his / her own business. Indeed, putting into practice the suggestions provided in this book will significantly improve readers' sales results and increase turnover, profits, customer loyalty, sometimes even unexpectedly.

Some of the techniques offered present a challenge to usual thought patterns of Western culture; however, have been and still are used (sometimes consciously, more often unconsciously) by some of the greatest scientists, olympic athletes, doctors, artists, managers the world has had. Well-known personalities (not only in their specific field) as Wolfgang A. Mozart, Thomas Edison, Albert Einstein, Wilma Rudolph, Laura Wilkinson, Emile Coue, Carl Simonton, Anne Mulcahy, Larry Page, Richard Bach, Charles Howard are among the most well known examples.

The emotional intelligence, the power of core beliefs, the awareness of the "computing power" of the unconscious part of the brain, along with the reprogramming of the traditional neural pathways of the mind, are able to provide tools that maximize the effectiveness of every sales rep. The development of a set of "sales tools" like enthusiasm, focus, determination, energy, self esteem, resilience, empathy, are able to grant long lasting sales excellence to all salespeople.

Finally, I must warn the reader of some facet of this book which openly contradicts what, until now, the reader himself has probably believed absolutely true. The advice is to read the book with an open mind, holding back any judgment about it, and applying carefully what it recommends. The results will pay off for many years to come.

2 - ACTIVITY OF UNCONSCIOUS MIND

A quick intuition; the desire to drink Coke instead of Pepsi; a sense of familiarity with a person never seen or known; the preference for Bmw instead of Mercedes; a sudden certainty of a decision to make; a major purchase made on impulse.

Apparently they are all unrelated events; however, they show a continuous and tight working of the unconscious mind, which through its continuous activity is able to influence in a sensible fashion the conscious decision-making processes and, therefore, actions, behaviors, responses to stimuli from external environment, and results.

Today, long after Sigmund Freud has spread his theory that behaviors are a consequence of mysterious memories and powerful unconscious drives, modern neuroscientists probe the depths of the mind and its mechanisms. Through sophisticated machinery they are able to provide precise images of neuronal cells that form the brain mass, and make available valuable information on the mechanisms (conscious and unconscious) influencing individuals' decisions and behaviors.

"Most of what we do every minute of life is unconscious," said Paul Whelan, a neuroscientist at the University of Wisconsin. In this pioneering lab the questions about how people behave and why, what they decide and how, what motivates and what does not, rather than be answered on a sofa by a psychoanalyst, are discovered through complex equipment, able to "read" the states of excitation of neurons cells in specific brain areas. This pioneering scientist has made evident the deep links between the activity of the brain that does not fall under the influence of the conscious mind and its behavior in daily activities.

Understanding the mechanisms that regulate the activity of the unconscious has deep implications for the life of people. At the same time, it is a challenge for all things that, until now, has been considered true. In fact what is today revealed by modern neurosciences looks like a revolution for the logical way of thinking, typical of the Western culture. Putting full trust in the logical processes of the intellect, assigning them the task of guiding all aspects of life, was one of the ways of thinking typical of French Enlightenment and Revolution. Still today, in the Western world, it is a very powerful belief. However, this deep faith in the adequacy of reason to solve problems of existence has been questioned by many scientific discoveries in the field of cognitive neurosciences, which today strongly support the idea that 95% of our mental activity is unconscious. Therefore most of our ideas, decisions, actions, emotions and behaviors depend on the 95% of mental activity that does not fall under the domain of our daylight consciousness.

For many years, researchers have been reluctant to further studies on the unconscious, especially for difficulties related in assigning scientific value to the results of laboratory tests. Today, times have changed. New paths for the systematic study of the unconscious have been developed, very different from the methods of classical psychoanalysis that put the patient on the couch, asking him to join voluntarily. The methodologies used today include sophisticated tools like fMRI (functional magnetic resonance imaging), the analysis of the basic processes of perception, learning and attention (exposing participants to very fast tests, which cannot be perceived by the conscious mind), and the advent of modern neurosciences (investigating the mechanisms of neuronal activation).

Through this research some of basic ideas of the Freudian theories have been confirmed; others, were refuted. In the first part of the last century, the unconscious was perceived as a sinister place of primordial conflicts. Lust, jealousy, failures, fears, anger, secret desires, and worse, were believed to be secretly held in a dark region of the mind, which starts just beyond our awareness. These impulses, sporadically emerging during dreaming, would be "invisible" to the daily awareness, and able to exert a much greater power than that of volition. Later, mainly thanks to Carl Jung (originally very close to Sigmund Freud) and his approach to psychoanalytic theories coupled with Eastern cultures, a growing number of researchers began to attach a meaning of spirituality and liberation to the unconscious mind.

For example, one of the essential premises of psychoanalysis - the fact that individuals possess unconscious defensive barriers appointed to preserve the self-esteem - has been largely confirmed. At the same time Freud's idea on the existence of a primitive and unconscious "child", was proven largely insufficient by laboratory tests: the unconscious is much more sophisticated and powerful than he had imagined. In this area, humans possess extraordinary abilities and powerful processes, critical at any behavioral level, and acting beyond the curtains of the conscious mind.

The adaptive unconscious

These processes, collectively termed as "adaptive unconscious" define the way in which we perceive the outside world, we deal with challenging situations, we relate with other individuals, we act a certain behavior, we set our own goals and act to achieve them. Many laboratory experiments have shown that most of the decisions depend from the adaptive unconscious, in practice the part of us that operates constantly, and with great speed and effectiveness, below the threshold of consciousness.

The adaptive unconscious is equipped with a "computing power" infinitely superior to that of the conscious mind (about 8,000 times greater), operates at several levels simultaneously, is not limited by the usual constraints of space / time, and thinks associatively and in a non-linear fashion. The adaptive unconscious makes it possible, for example, to perform a turn in the car without having to face a series of complex calculations regarding the speed of the vehicle, the turning radius, the distance from the curb, the adhesion factor of the tires, and so on.

Adaptive unconscious helps in the selection of products to buy, often relieving the conscious mind from complex and lengthy evaluations about usefulness, price / quality ratio, seriousness and reliability of the brand, diffusion and safety of the product itself.

Adaptive unconscious is also what causes us to have full confidence in a stranger, without having to linearly analyze every move he makes, every word he utters, the exact intonation of his speech, the details of the clothing he wears, the coherence that emerges by comparing his verbal and nonverbal language. All these aspects are evaluated simultaneously and at multiple levels, generating faster attraction or repulsion for the "unknown" under consideration.

Timothy Wilson (professor of psychology at the University of Virginia) in his well-known book (Strangers to ourselves) provides an assessment of the unconscious neither good nor bad, and even not particularly spiritual. Its role would simply be to help in the decisions and behaviors related to everyday life.

Wilson shows that this unconscious force handles most of the processes of "lower" level that occur without awareness, and he defines the unconscious as that set of mental processes that are inaccessible to consciousness, but that influence the daily decisions. However, Wilson argues, we must not make the mistake of believing that unconscious is like an automaton or a "homunculus". In a chapter titled "Who's in Charge?" Wilson notes that unconscious appears to play a central role in taking important decisions, such as those relating to the job, to the right person to marry, to how to raise the children and if, even in the heat of the moment, whether it's really a good idea to publicly point out the shortcomings of own boss.

In addition, regarding the chain thinking - acting (the action follows the thought that generates it) Wilson offers a fascinating twist: both would be originated and preceded by an unconscious process (cause) which in turn gives rise to a conscious thought (first effect) that finally leads to action (second effect). It would be only the apparent temporal coordination between conscious thought and action (both at conscious level) that gives the illusion that the action is only daughter of the conscious thought.

One of the privileged fields for the application of these concepts is surely represented by sales. Nowadays it's a complex activity that can not be separated (neither from vendor side, nor from that of customer) by a series of unconscious processes which, in compliance with the 95 % / 5% rule, determine sales success, well beyond the sales techniques consciously used.

Often it is believed that by applying effective but traditional sales techniques sales success should arrive by default. While not contesting the validity of that saying (sales superstars must necessarily master effective sales techniques to achieve a long lasting success) the traditional sales techniques represent only 5% of salespeople's potential: sales excellence is achieved by using at least a fraction of the additional 95% of "super-powers".

The great thing is that everything is needed to improve is already possessed by each salesman, who just need to learn how to "govern" and use it to his fullest advantage. The enormous "computing power" that unconscious mind already holds has to be harnessed and used to achieve sales excellence. The subsequent parts of this book will explore the unconscious mechanisms that allow salespeople to:

• Harness at any time their most powerful mental and physical energy

• Acquire the highest authoritativeness and behavioral consistency in front of the customer;

• Strengthen their sales action far beyond their current expectations;

• Reaching their sales targets in any competitive environment, even the most harsh.

All that will come through an analysis about how core beliefs act, how to nurture own emotional intelligence, how to avoid self-sabotaging behaviors, how to reprogram the brain's neuronal paths. And at this point a question is due: how to take full advantage of the knowledge gained reading this book?

Coming to the end of this book, readers will find that the best way to trigger an increase in their sales results is to adopt a "fitymi" approach (fake it till you make it). Exactly as Robert Gilder (a famous Uk artists manager) is used to say: "Act the way you want to become, and you will become the way you act". This simply rule suggests to act as if you were already the sales superstar you want to become. Therefore, those who want to achieve sales excellence think, behave, act as if they had already achieved excellence. So doing, they will obtain the maximum consistency between objectives and behaviors. The rest of this book will prove (through examples and exercises) how to reprogram the mind to achieve sales greatness.

Before ending this chapter, I wish to offer readers a final thought: major achievements are always the result of strong commitment. Through the use of this book salespeople will be able to achieve extraordinary sales results, providing they are willing to make the recommended exercises. Without an investment in time, energy and efforts salespeople will go nowhere. Who doesn't want to "get hands dirty" abandon the reading, now.

3 - HOW THE MIND WORKS

Among the most powerful computers in the world, for the 4th consecutive time, China's massive Tianhe-2 supercomputer, aka "Milky Way-2", has retained the top spot as the world's fastest supercomputer, according to a biannual Top500 list of supercomputers. That's no surprise, Tianhe-2, developed by China's National University of Defense Technology (NUDT,) can operate at 33,86 petaflops per second (Pflop/s), or 33,860 quadrillion calculations per second, cost approximately $390 million and is made by thousands of Intel Xeon E5-2692v2 12C 2.2GHz processors. The National Supercomputer Center in Guangzhou (south China), where Tianhe-2 is installed, it is also reported to make an update to increase the system's speed to over 100 Plops/s.

Short ago it was announced the US plan on spending $325 million to build two supercomputers which will be three to five times faster than the Tianhe-2 system. Anyway Titan, installed at the Department of Education in the Oak Ridge National Laboratory, remains the No. 2 system with a performance of 17.59 Pflop/s.

The Sequoia, installed at the DOE's Lawrence Livermore National Laboratory, is again the No. 3 system with a performance of 17.17 Pflop/s.

Japan's K computer is the No. 4 system with 10.51 Pflop/s, followed by Mira, installed at the DOE's Argonne National Laboratory, which has a performance of 8.59 Pflop/s, which sits at No. 5.

I could continue this way for long however, in terms of flexibility and ability to learn, these machines are far exceeded by the human brain, a wonderful and powerful device, of which all of us possess a unique piece, a kind of prototype. This perfect machine, with an almost unlimited potential, with a small supply of fuel (oxygen of the blood and a bit of glucose) has the ability to process and store an incredible volume of information, much more than any supercomputer.

Typically people do not know so much about its operation; therefore, in this section, I propose a fascinating journey to discover this magnificent machine, without going into too much detail (deeply explain how the brain is made and operates would be a very complex topic, for which I refer you to specialized books) but without omitting anything that could be useful to really understand what computing power's miracle we all hold. Understanding the basic mechanisms of the human brain can lead to understand how important it is, indeed crucial, in everyday life. Even more important, how we can learn to use it in the best possible way.

First of all let's start by saying that the brain is our operation center: it receives signals from the sensory system (ears, hands, tongue, eyes ...) and sends commands to the different parts of the body. In its way of working looks like the CPU of a computer or like the cockpit of an aircraft and, like these are composed by chips and wires, our brain is made by neurons and nerve fibers. Neurons operate as many small independent computers (in a parallel architecture) that process information from the senses and send the appropriate commands to the body parts. Neurons (about 100 billion) are connected through approximately 160 Km of nerve fibers, that carry on the nervous signals. Each neuron communicates with its neighbors (approximately 100,000) in less than 20 milliseconds (one tenth of the time it takes to blink an eye).

This extraordinary computing power makes neurons able to tackle a task at virtually the same instant. This allows, for example, to recognize a familiar face in less than half a second, to play chess, or to fly a supersonic jet.

Left and right hemispheres

At cortex level, the brain shows a split between right and left hemisphere, which correspond to different functions and specializations. This idea comes directly from Freud's psychoanalytic theory, and nowadays it is considered just a working hypothesis. In fact the difference should be made in relation to the different levels of which the brain mass is composed (reptilian, limbic system, neocortex) however, for simplicity, I will follow Freud's indications.

The left hemisphere is rational, practical, logical, linear, analytical, mathematical. It handles calculus, language, logical thinking. It controls the right side of the body. The right hemisphere is emotional, creative, imaginative, childlike, intuitive, timeless, spaceless, holistic. It handles creativity, associative thinking, intuition, emotions. It controls the left side of the body. The two hemispheres are joined by the corpus callosum, and communicate through it.

The left hemisphere, the logic one, is ideally identified as the conscious mind, detects facts and then processes informations that are subject to a cause and effect relationship. It handles its host (the body) with a long term horizon. The right hemisphere, the emotional one, is associated with the unconscious mind instead, and handles all biochemical aspects of the body, and follows a short term view.

As a general rule, during states of waking, the ego relies more to the left hemisphere; otherwise, the right hemisphere takes over during oniric phases.

The specialization of the hemispheres

The two hemispheres do not show the same power in driving our thoughts, behavior and physiology. From a study of the 60's by George A. Miller (an US cognitive psychologist) sprang the rule of "seven plus or minus two" relatively to the left hemisphere. That means we have available, at any particular moment, from 5 to 9 units of conscious attention. Similar studies showed that the right hemisphere is able to handle, at the same time, more than 63,000 different activities, mostly unconscious (glandular processes, blood circulation, respiration, biochemical balance, instinctive movements and reactions, emotions, and so forth). Miller's theory supports the idea that, considering 100 the leading power of our brain, 5% relies on the conscious part, 95% on the unconscious one. Therefore, the unconscious mind seems to be endowed with a huge potential, almost unlimited. Basically it acts as if it were our autopilot.

Programs of unconscious mind

Like any computer, also our unconscious mind needs instructions to work properly. Its instructions, following the pc's analogy, can be seen like programs. They are represented by our experience, our ideas about the world and about ourselves, our beliefs, and partly come from genetic inheritance.

Just like a computer, our brain has the bios (basic input output system) ideally represented by the genetic instructions; has an operating system (instructions partly genetic and partly experiential); use applications (programs completely tied to life experiences). The moment we decide to provide a command to our

20

right hemisphere with the aim of achieving a certain result, we must take account of the following basic rules.

1) Right hemisphere is literal, childish and uncritical

2) Right hemisphere is categorical and self-validating

3) Right hemisphere does not immediately recognize negatives (no, not)

4) Right hemisphere confuses reality with fantasy.

Let's see, in practice, what that means, in terms of behaviors.

Right hemisphere is literal, childish and uncritical. This means that it doesn't like to make calculations, proposals, test theories, or evaluate the pros and cons of something: it takes things exactly as we provide them to it. It certainly happened to many, coming back home in the evening, to leave the car keys in a place different from the usual drawer. The morning after, looking into the drawer, the keys don't show up. Then a frantic search begins, while the keys are lying in plain sight on a shelf. After many minutes of breathlessness investigation without finding the keys (they are still in view, on the shelf) finally they are detected. Why is that? Probably because the command sent to the right hemisphere has been: "... I always put the keys in the drawer..." This process works with the car keys and, of course, with everything else.

A typical case is linked to self-sabotaging ideas about own abilities. If I am filled with ideas of inadequacy in performing a certain task, I will experience considerable resistance in executing it; viceversa, if I'm sure to succeed, the unconscious will act on an empowering idea, leading my action towards success. So, please, be careful in making consideration on yourself: every word you say and every thought you have can be received like commands by the right hemisphere, and probably it will do its utmost to fully execute them.

Right hemisphere is categorical and self-validating. Unconscious thoughts tend to see everything black or white, without considering any nuances. Like or dislike, good or bad, right or wrong, and so on. In addition, the right hemisphere tends to suppress or ignore the facts that might disprove its beliefs, instead accepting completely what confirms them. Beliefs of conscious mind are mainly experiential: a new plain fact can disprove an old belief, replacing it with another. The unconscious mind, on the other side, considers its beliefs absolutely true, and therefore rejects any evidence to the contrary. It 'easy to see how this, in the sale, may represent an area of quite high risk.

Right hemisphere does not immediately recognize negatives (no, not). Although there are a few exceptions, in almost all cases, the right hemisphere does not recognize negatives adverbs, and does not obey the commands that contain them. If I ask you not to think, I underline it, not to think of the moon, what would happen? In your mind, would immediately appear a moon image! Why? Just because the brain does not accept, in the first instance, the negative terms.

So "I will not smoke anymore" is turned into its contrary, "not eating" becomes eating, "not fighting" becomes fighting, and so on. How many times we promised ourselves, even with a high dose of conviction, not to do something any longer? Well, who did it, has probably noticed that, despite the great strength of will, the bad behavior popped up again, many times.

It largely depends from the way the right hemisphere reads commands coming from the volition, skipping negative adverbs. And also, the higher the pressure of the will to discontinue the bad habit, the more it recurs. Using negative adverbs provides the unconscious mind with a command which is contrary to the intentions of the conscious will. Also this fact, in sales, is an outbreak of problems. So, please do remember that the instructions to the right hemisphere should be sent in an affirmative way.

Right hemisphere confuses fantasy with reality. For it, thinking and acting are almost the same thing. For example: I ask you to imagine in front of you a big ice cream, which gives off a heady scent. I ask you also to imagine to hold it with one hand and begin to voluptuously lick it, savoring its sweetness. While you savor it, enjoy its coolness in your mouth. Later, when it is almost finished, you get back to the ice cream shop to buy another one. But what happens? Do you get your mouth watering? Of course you do, and the reason is that the right brain is skilled in evocations and does not, in principle, make distinctions between reality and fantasy!

It is sufficient to imagine the act to enjoy an icecream to activate, at least partially, the series of physiological processes that would be triggered if you had really eaten the icecream. Just for this reason, if we imagine to encounter issues in performing a given task, these issues will probably pop up; conversely, if we think vividly, concretely, emotionally, about ourselves in the act of successfully accomplish the same task, chances of success will increase a lot.

There is scientific and empirical evidence that intensely visualizing a given behavior, activates the same physiological effects (with a slightly reduced intensity) of when you concretely make that action. Just remember that, for example, when we dwell on thoughts or memories that evoke intense emotional waves (similar to those experienced in real situation) our physiology changes. Respiratory and heart rates increase, process of sweating begins, pupils dilate more, muscle tone increases, glands release adrenaline and noradrenaline to prepare our body to action.

These quirks in unconscious mind behavior can be used in full at any time, as long as instructions sent to the subconscious part of the brain comply with the needed syntax. In doing so, the enormous power of the unconscious brain can be put at the fingertips of sales activity. In the last part of the book I will describe how to properly use methods and syntax to reprogram the neural pathways, in so rewiring the brain.

4 - EMOTIONAL INTELLIGENCE

The last decade of the twentieth century saw a proliferation of scientific studies about people's emotions. That was also made possible by innovative machines, including equipment for fMRI and computer-aided electroencephalography with 256 sensors. These technologies, which allow to obtain images of brain activity of a living individual, have provided a mass of neurobiological data that allow scientists to understand more clearly how the emotional centers of the brain push us to tears or joy, to fear or courage, to hatred or love. These data constitute a real challenge for those who support a conception of intelligence limited to IQ (rational intelligence quotient) and believe that success in sales (and, more generally, in life) largely comes from this skill.

The rational intelligence quotient is a score obtained from one of the tests to measure it, and is expressed as the ratio of the mental age (defined by the test itself) divided by the chronological age. For example, in a child with a mental age of 12 years and chronological age of 10, the result of IQ is as follows: (12/10) x 100, or 120. The italian-french psychologist Alfredo Binetti (his name was later changed to Alfred Binet), around 1905, published the first modern rational intelligence test, known as "Binet - Simon intelligence scale". From that time, many other tests were presented, both for children and adults (Wisc, Wais, Wais III, and others).

These tests have almost all in common their structure, which typically requires the solution of a number of logic problems. For example, the Wais III, among the most common IQ tests, consists of 14 tests, 7 time-bounded (information, understanding, arrangement of numbers and letters, digits memory, vocabulary, similarities, arithmetic reasoning) and 7 focusing to logic skills (coding digits and symbols, completion of images, block design, Raven's matrices, picture arrangement, and others).

A very interesting study was made in California, in which Richard Haier, professor of psychology at the Department of Pediatrics at the University of California, with some of his colleagues at the University of New Mexico, has done a fMRI test to obtain structural images of the brain of a panel of men, while they were submitted to an IQ test. The study has shown that human logic intelligence appears to be based on a portion of gray matter of the brain. That test has also shown just about 6% of the total gray matter mass seems to be activated during the execution of these tasks, and so can be related to IQ.

In addition, Howard Gardner (an Harvard psychology professor) has identified at least 10 different kind of intelligences, in addition to the well- known logic one. Among them spatial, musical, kinesthetic, ethic, emotional.

Peter Salovey (an US social psychologist, current President at Yale University), along with Daniel Goleman (another US psychologist and best-sellers author) are probably the most expert psychologists living today about the branch of psychology named emotional intelligence. They define it a form of intelligence that allows people to feel emotions and use them consciously in relationship with others and with themselves. A score, defined EQ (emotional quotient) shows the possession of a certain degree of emotional intelligence.

The possession of a high rate of EQ affect the behavior of its possessor and, through social interactions, also that of his interlocutor. A high EQ allows those who have it to make themselves more desirable from the surrounding environment. In fact, the measure of IQ shows its limitations when used as an index for predicting success degree (which is defined as satisfying and fulfilling life and job) that a given individual will get during his life. It has been proven that individuals with a high IQ are often showing modest or even poor social behaviors, and good life success cannot be separated from effective social behaviors.

On the other side, effective social behaviors often lead to receive high social acceptance and establish strong relationships with own social environment (relatives, peers, friends, colleagues, customers, and so on). All that is a surefire way for reaching a high life quality. Needless to repeat that effective social behaviors are linked with high EQ's.

A famous series of articles, published in the late 90's by the Harvard Business Review, showed that:

• EQ alone is responsible for about 60% of cases of professional success;

• 90% of top performers (sales, management) hold a high EQ;

• Less than 20% of low performers hold a high EQ.

In addition, a series of studies conducted in the United States at the beginning of the new century have discovered important relationships between a high EQ and sales success.

• A portion of the sales network of Hallmark Communities, which received specific training sessions about emotional intelligence, generated 25% profits increase compared to colleagues to whom the training had not been delivered (Broadberry, 2003);

- In AT & T, 91% of the sales managers with the best performance were holding a high EQ (Broadberry, 2002);

- L'Oreal realized over $ 91,000 in additional yearly sales (compared to traditional salespeople) from those reps selected according to their high EQ (Cherniss, 2003);

Another study was conducted, in 2011, by Johnson & Johnson, on more than three hundred managers about existing correlation from high managerial effectiveness and high EQ possession. Study showed that the most effective managers (especially in sales jobs) were those best equipped with a high EQ (Cavallo & Brienza, 2001). In fact, the greater need for emotional intelligence occurs in those jobs that, by their nature, must interact with other individuals and therefore make the interpersonal relationship a key success factor.

There are also other reasons why a high EQ facilitates achieving sales success. Some other US studies show that most of our choices and decisions are not only the result of a logic pros and cons thinking: in many cases, the rational faculties would be flanked by the emotional apparatus, which would constitute a "shortened path", able of making people reach a proper decision in a shorter time than that required by following a logical thinking about alternatives screening.

Emotional component involved in decisions would be decisive in cases where these relate to our person or relatives / peers close to us. To prove this thesis, Antonio Damasio (one of the best-known living neuroscientists) reports cases of some patients who, due to neurological damage suffered in brain areas devoted to emotions, had become completely unable to make a decision, despite being perfectly capable to fairly and rationally assess all involved factors. EQ (and related emotions) are therefore fundamental in decision-making, as well as interaction between individuals. Sales process, the success of which is by far a son of relationship that is established between seller and buyer (except, sometimes, cases of monopolistic markets) is perhaps the workplace par excellence in which a high EQ is a safe passport to high performances. EQ discovery therefore allows to answer questions like "Why some salesmen with high IQ get mediocre results, while others with a modest IQ manage to achieve excellence?".

The components of EQ

Concept of emotional intelligence, already described by Howard Gardner in two forms, intrapersonal and interpersonal skills, consists of several very important parts that support (in most cases unconsciously) mental health and psychosocial well-being, as well as professional performances. EQ was further developed in its multiple components and practical consequences by Daniel Goleman, who distinguishes two main subcategories:
-*Personal skills*, referring to the ability to catch different aspects of own emotional life;
-*Social skills*, relating to the manner in which we understand each other and we relate to other people.

Personal skills

Includes self-awareness, which leads us give a name and a meaning to our lives, and helps us understand emotional circumstances and causes that impact it; more generally, it allows a self-assessment of own skills and purposes so as to be able to set realistic goals, then choosing the most adequate personal resources to reach them. Also self-control is part of personal skills. It implies ability to recognize and control own emotions, which does not mean denying or suffocate them, but express them in socially acceptable forms. The inability to manage own emotions can, in fact, lead to act inappropriately, and perhaps exaggerated forms of aggression towards others, offering an unflattering self image. Who is in control of himself, usually manages to behave in a manner appropriate to given situation, taking into account the rules of social life, recognizing own responsibilities and mistakes, respecting his commitments and thus fulfilling the tasks / roles assigned.

Among the personal skills can be also placed the ability to feed own motivation, keeping it at a fair level even in the face of hassles or when things get difficult, and do not go as planned or hoped. The ability to self-motivate is composed by a fair dose of optimism and spirit of initiative, that push to pursue own goals, actively reacting to failures and frustrations. This last aspect, in sales, is of particular importance because sometimes, in the absence of short term success, salespeople get demotivated. This occurs above all because a weak business is often associated to ideas of professional inadequacy, incompetence, lack of experience. These judgments, in the unconscious, work hard and become the driver of self sabotaging decisions and behaviors.

Who, conversely, is in possession of a good degree of self-motivation has learned not to consider the so-called failure as a lack of professional skills, but just as a plain information on what doesn't work and must be avoided, to finally get the success the next time. This, for sales people, come from analyzing the reasons behind the negative result and deriving key information on what should be done and avoided, in the future, in order to facilitate the achievement of the expected result.

Social skills

They consist of set of features allowing us positively relate with others and constructively interact with them. One of the most important components of this area of emotional intelligence consists of empathy, or the ability to recognize emotions and feelings in other people, ideally putting ourselves in their shoes and being able to understand their points of view, interests and inner difficulties. Being empathetic means to perceive inner world of others as if it were our own, while maintaining awareness of their possible difference compared to our points of view.

Ability to effectively communicate, another social skill, is the ability to talk to others, making sure that the explicit content of the messages (sent by the words) is consistent with own beliefs and emotions (unwittingly revealed through body language). Communicate effectively is also being able to ask questions and listen, focusing also to emotional responses of our interlocutors. In addition also other skills like leadership (the ability to motivate and lead others) and assertiveness (the ability to balance own needs with those of others) are key components of social skills. According to Goleman, emotional intelligence can be developed through proper training, mainly directed to capture the feelings and emotions of the people surrounding us. Intelligence related to IQ tends to stabilize after the puberty age (to slowly begin to decline in the years of maturity), emotional intelligence can be improved in the course of an entire lifetime.

How EQ helps the sale

At this point it is legitimate to ask why emotions play a so key role in success (personal and professional) especially in field of sales. Neuroscientists and sociobiologists respond that the reason stems from the fact that, in social activities (sales surely enter in this category) we had been "programmed" in a way often allowing heart to complement mind and, sometimes, even prevailing. In other words, when a part of the person (usually the unconscious) feels that the decision he is about to take is important, asks to emotions for a support.

Scientists argue that our emotions guide us in addressing situations too complex and important for being entrusted to intellect alone (IQ). As everyone from his own experience knows, when it is time that decisions and actions take shape, feelings count at least as much (if not more) than rational thought. For example, in purchasing process (the higher the value of the asset in question the more the following dynamic intensifies) decision is often made on a base of emotional drives, and then rationally justified. Buying an asset like a winter house on Alps, for instance, probably makes the buyer be driven by unconscious thoughts, which in turn are feeded by emotions:

• I will possess a house in the mountains, as my rich friend does (envy)

• Buying this house will allow me to show greater wealth (ostentation)

• If I can afford it, it means that I have achieved success (pride)

• I will make my girlfriend happy (love)

After the decision is made (mainly from unconscious-emotional mind) the conscious mind usually looks for hard facts to justify it.

• The price per sq.m. is very good

- The prestige of that city is increasing

- In the long run, I'll save money compared to the hotel

- It's very close to the ski slopes

EQ, which is manifested largely unconsciously, sculpt behavior of individuals, impacting on aspects such as listening skills, talking skills, consideration for others, relationship management, cooperation, failure recover, perseverance in pursuing goals, decisions making. All these behaviors play a key role in the sales process, which often base its success on the ability to establish a good relationship between two or more people. At a conscious level, good sales results are pursued by means conscious use of "rational" tools (sales techniques). That probably helps for about 5% of the entire "sales power" of salesman. Sales excellence is reached using the remaining 95% of sales potential, including typical tools of emotional intelligence.

5 - CORE BELIEFS

Usually the term belief is defined as a feeling of certainty about something. Each person possesses certainties about some aspects of life, which result from an accumulation of circumstances and previous experience. However, the meaning of the term goes beyond this, since beliefs are not just a product of thought. In fact, they represent much more than what people think is true: they represent the foundations of what people can (or can't) get from their private or professional life.

What a person believes is the result of a series of oaths, promises and validations made with himself, and impacts on every part of the individual (emotions, body, mind, consciousness). Beliefs, at times, rely on an objective factual basis (for example, the belief that human beings are not able to fly like birds because they don't have wings), but often they comes from entirely subjective mental processes (for example, the belief that the number 13 brings good or bad luck). For example, a belief fairly shared at the time of Christopher Columbus was that the earth was flat and that, sailing far beyond the Gibraltar Strait, created the risk of falling down; another belief, widespread in much more recent times in the sports world, was alleged inability to fall under 4 minutes to run a classic distance, the mile.

These powerful behavior's drivers influence the actions of both individuals and entire populations, and often prevent accessing best resources and achieve best results. In fact, until 1492, in Southern Europe, the fear of reaching the end of the earth's surface and then fall into the void has prevented discovering new lands on other continents. In athletics, believing that it was impossible to go below a certain time has prevented many athletes to grasp the deserved success.

Why do beliefs exist

What is the purpose of these forms of thought? Why they are there? What do they aim to? Answering these questions urges us to analyze their usefulness in terms of survival. The mind, like any other computer to properly work, in addition to being equipped with effective programs, must be continuously feeded by datas. Our five senses (sight, hearing, taste, smell, touch) provides the input of those informations that are within the reach of the senses. These informations allow the mind to develop strategies to enable the individual, first to survive, secondly to get close to pleasure and away from pain.

If the sense of sight detects a hazard (a sudden obstacle on the highway) automatically the mind processes a series of actions that allow the individual to avoid that danger (pushing brake, steering left). If the sense of smell detects a bad scent (the meat is rotten) the mind develops an alternative strategy compared to the swallowing previously programmed, and the meat is thrown in the trash basket.

The five senses, of course, are used to detect stimuli that are within their reach: over certain distances smell, sight and hearing doesn't work; if there is no physical contact, touch and taste are not able to send signals to the brain. It is therefore necessary that the place in which a signal is available be within the reach of the sensory system, otherwise the latter is unable to detect the signal.

Another barrier to the collection of data from the environment is represented by the time factor. This means that the data must be detectable at the time when they are actually available. The senses, in most cases, can not detect data from past or future: the sense of sight can just detects events which are contemporary to the observation time.

Some technological innovations (telescope, telegraph, phone, radio, TV, internet) are indeed intended to overcome the constraints of space and time, allowing the human mind to detect signals out from the detectable horizon. Our brain, in order to maximize the chances of survival, has always used another tool: core beliefs. Unconscious mind treats core beliefs as a kind of mental map that represents those parts of the world with which there isn't a sensory contact, and uses them to integrate data collected by the senses themselves. This allows the individual to successfully move on unknown territories, far from senses' reach.

The belief that wild beasts were used to drink at a river during night time (the river being out of reach of the senses prevented the presence of wild animals from being detected visually, acoustically, olfactory, kinesthetically) probably saved the lives of many hominids, in prehistoric times. Checking directly (visually, acoustically, olfactory, kinesthetically) whether was dangerous or not go to the river at night, wouldn't allowed our ancestors to live long.

Thus, in more recent times, the girl who parked the car in the car park of the house, would not be able to find it anymore, only relying on the support of her senses. For her sensory apparatus, the car has even ceased to exist, because none of the five senses is able to detect it. The ability to find the car is therefore entrusted to the belief that it is still in the car park.

Sensorial data and beliefs have been designed to work independently from one another (although, in certain cases, beliefs originate from data collected by the sensory system). From all above comes that the full value of beliefs, as a mean of survival, can not be separated from an almost total rejection of any evidence to the contrary, even if supported by incontrovertible facts.

So unconscious mind tends to reject any item that calls into question its core beliefs; otherwise, if it would be possible to continuously change the belief systems as a function of experiential data collected each time, the system itself would lose all effectiveness, as a solid system that can facilitate survival.

In fact, if the belief in the presence of a dangerous animal every time the grass swayed had been challenged (evaluating the presence of wind, or waiting to be able to check with smell, hearing or sight) ancestors of the human race probably wouldn't had the chance to populate the planet with about 7 billion human beings.

Once a belief is originated, acquires a strong character of impermeability to any evidence to the contrary, becoming therefore extremely resistant to any change. This aspect explains why, often, some people hold absurd beliefs, contradicted by facts, and nevertheless manifest resistance to change them.

Moreover, since the beliefs systems holds thousand, maybe millions beliefs, all interconnected, the removal of even one belief only risks to generate a discontinuity in these thoughts patterns. So, at a deep level, the removal tends to be prevented by the unconscious mind.

Beliefs effectiveness

These unconscious instructions act like real pc programs, influence each other and affect people behavior. The ways in which core beliefs influence the behavior of individuals are not recognized by the conscious mind, and are very effective, as they use 95% of the potential that is available at the fingertips of unconscious mind. Therefore, guided by their beliefs, people are able to put in place very persevering behavioral strategies (that's why they are very effective) able to change (or create, or delete) objective facts.

An example of this is placebo effect, which relies on the belief that a certain drug can bring benefit. A precursor of the placebo effect was a French pharmacist, Emile Coue. Exercising his profession as a pharmacist, Emile Coue had indeed observed the enormous power of beliefs. Handing over a drug to his patients, he was used to say: "You'll see, this will certainly heal you". And later: "It is just the beginning; you'll improve day by day" Healing often occurred with drugs without real pharmacological effect.

A well-known case, reported in many medical textbooks, is related to an anticancer drug, widely discussed and with fluctuating fortunes, Krebiozen, imported in the United States around the 50's. In the tests carried over by the FDA (Food and Drug Administration) was involved an oncologist named Bruno Klopfer, who had a patient (Mr. Wright) with a severe form of cancer to the lymph nodes. All traditional therapies had already been used without success, and Wright was considered terminally ill, with a few days of life. His neck, armpits, chest, groin showed tumors the size of an orange, and every day was necessary to drain from tumors almost a liter of liquid, to enable him to survive.

When Wright accidentally learned of existence of Krebiozen, deepened the topic, and asked with great insistence to Dr. Klopfer to immediately be submitted to treatment. Dr. Klopfer Initially refused, since the drug was not tested yet, but after a while, and considering Wright already doomed, he agreed. First treatment was carried out on a Friday, and the following Monday Dr.Klopfer had a huge surprise: he saw Wright standing up, walking down the hospital hall. Klopfer reported that tumor masses "were shrunken like snow in the sun" and reduced by more than half.

Within some days after the first treatment the patient was able to leave the hospital and, as doctors were able to observe, without any cancer's symptoms. Wright went on a normal life for a while until, in a newspaper, an article questioned Krebiozen's effectiveness. Wright got deeply depressed, symptoms of the disease reappeared, and he had to be readmitted to the hospital. At that point Dr. Klopfer decided to try a very bold experiment: he told his patient that the effectiveness of the substance could not be questioned, and that failure of some pharmacological test was due to some samples of corrupted drug. He kept saying that he had a quantity of Krebiozen highly concentrated, and offered to resume the treatment. In fact Dr. Klopfer had in mind to treat Wright with simple distilled water, enriched with neutral substances. Again the result was astonishing: tumors shrank, and in a short time Wright resumed his normal life.

After a few months, AMA (American Medical Association) published a new report which definitively confirmed Krebiozen was devoid of any therapeutic value. This time the confidence of Wright was completely destroyed, his illness took control again and, in the end, took him to the grave.

Another case cited by the psychiatric literature, is the case of a woman, suffering from splitted personality, who periodically believed to be plagued by a severe form of diabetes. When schizophrenia gave her a bit of respite, she was a normal person, acting as such; when he turned his mind on being diabetics, his blood sugar level spurted to typical values of advanced forms of diabetes, to return to normal when she weren't affected by her schizophrenia.

These two facts contain extraordinary information: the belief system of an individual is powerful enough to generate impressive physiological changes, even up to the spontaneous remission of tremendous diseases, and their disappearance, or viceversa.

A different case comes directly from the sports world. For decades it was believed that the record of the 100-meter dash could not reach 10" net: common reasons were found in the athlete's physiology, the cardiovascular system, strength of the tendons, the respiratory rhythm. In fact, this limit was not reached by anyone for a long time. We remember Americans Tolan, Jarvis, Tewksbury, British Lee, Atcherley, Beaton, Belgian De Re, Swedesh Andersson and Westergren, Canadian Williams and many more great athletes, who tried to reach 10 "net, but in vain. The widespread belief was that the 10" were an impassable limit.

June 21st, 1960, during Roma's Olympic Games the German athlete Armin Hary was the first in history to run 100-meter dash in 10" net. Suddenly, as if by miracle, other athletes equaled his performance: Canadian Harry Jerome (07/15/60), Venezuelan Horacio Esteves, Americans Robert Lee Hayes and James Ray Hines. Demolished this seemingly insurmountable barrier, in a short time many sprinters in the world were able to run the 100-meter dash in 10 "net.

This story suggests how the limiting influence of general beliefs can act, and how it literally represents a barrier to harnessing the best physical and psychic energies. Once shown that "you could do it", by changing a belief rooted in the sports world, many athletes automatically managed to achieve a result that until then was considered impossible to achieve. Feeling the task within the reach of an athlete, albeit well prepared, suddenly allowed many of them to unlock their physical and psychic resources, making such performance possible. Resources that, until then, had not been used.

As seen from the examples above, there are limiting beliefs (that limit what one can get) and empowering beliefs (that amplify what one can get). Without encroaching into metaphysics, it can be said that the results that people get are a direct function of what they expect to get. In other words, you can formulate a general rule concerning beliefs: what you expect tends to be realized.

The use of own potential

Every human being has a certain potential (mental and physical resources), and the results obtained in almost all tasks are the direct result of the use of this potential. However, the success doesn't so much depend on the size of the possessed potential (each individual possesses an huge amount of it, well beyond what is normally considered possible) but from the way it is used. The way to use it is governed by the belief system.

Examples of limiting beliefs are observable in humans, as well as in animals. An example that comes from the animal world, is on capture and domestication of elephants. The training of these mighty animals, once captured, begins with a period spent with the legs chained to huge buried piles, not allowing them the slightest movement. After several days of frantic and powerful attempts to break free, in the absence of food and water the animal, completely exhausted, capitulates. Realizing the complete uselessness to free itself from the bonds, it decides to accept the fact of being unable to move.

From then the domestication begins. The trainer starts to move the animal, warily, and guiding it with a grappling hook; simultaneously rewards the good behaviors with food and water, completing the conditioning. When the training is completed, to prevent the animal from escaping, the trainer simply tie it with a string to a pole or a tree: the belief that the noose to the leg does not allow it to get away is now so deeply rooted, that the elephant does not even attempt to recover that freedom from which it is separated only by a very weak piece of string. These rules apply also in sales: if you do not believe you can succeed, it is likely that you will fail; conversely, if you believe you can accomplish a certain task (within the same scenario) the odds in your favor increase a lot.

An interesting confirmation of the practical consequences of a belief is from the so-called "Thomas theorem", coming from an US sociologist (W.L.Thomas) that, in the first half of the last century, ruled that "...when someone defines a situation as real, it becomes real in its consequences". In other words, the arbitrary interpretation of a fact (a belief) is powerful enough to determine objective events that confirm it. Thomas also asserted that a number of beliefs (called "situations") are able to fully influence the plan of life of individuals and their own personality. A classic example is the belief that a bank is going to bankrupt. If many people ripen the (unproven) belief that their bank is going to fail, would rush to withdraw their savings, thus causing the failure in the reality, even though the fundamentals of the crisis had been only speculations unsupported by objective facts. From the Thomas theorem descended the so-called "self-fulfilling prophecies" (as defined by US sociologist R.K.Merton).

At its beginning, the self-fulfilling prophecy is an unproven definition of a situation that calls for a new behavior which, acted, makes the initial postulate real. Just to give an idea of the dynamics of that, let me use an extreme example: consider a false and offensive judgment, by the individual A to the individual B. Although not supported by facts, expressed violently and suddenly, a sentence like: "You're an aggressive person!" would trigger a wave of anger in individual B, who could attack A, thus validating the initial definition.

All this has an impact not only on private lives of people, but also in professional one, sometimes contributing to sediment strongly disempowering beliefs. Typical self-limiting beliefs are the following:

• That guy possesses certain traits, abilities, skills, which make me down him;

• We are not able to succeed, therefore it is useless to grope;

• That opinion is correct, then there are no other interpretations;

• At this problem can only apply a given solution, therefore it is useless to look for other ways to solve it.

Consciously, and especially in sales activity, not being able to complete a certain task is usually justified without challenging any underlying disempowering belief (people aren't aware of them). The failure is then motivated with a series of excuses/alibis (logical, consistent and seemingly justified) that explain the reasons of the lack of success. Unfortunately, often excuses / alibis have nothing to do with the real underlying reason (the self-limiting belief) that is the real cause of the ineffective behavior.

From my experience in having managed many sales networks, small and large (from a few units in niche markets to large teams of several hundreds reps in consumer markets) I would like to extrapolate a series of alibis, among those most frequently used in an attempt to justify a poor performance.

- Market is too difficult for us

- Competitor X is more flexible than we are

- Prices of competition are lower than ours

- Customers have become very difficult to please

- Our competitors sell better products than ours

- Our terms are too short

- Quality of our products is too poor

- Our competitors make a greater advertising pressure

The role of core beliefs in the sales results

All above, applied to the world of sales, makes very clear that an important part of results that a rep gets is a function of his core beliefs about his skills, type of customer, product's quality, support provided by his own company, competition, and so forth. These beliefs translate into unconscious behaviors that facilitate or make it difficult to finalize the sales call, often regardless from level of experience and skills possessed by the salesman.

In one of my previous jobs, years ago, I had the role of sales & marketing director in a B2B company selling durable goods. For a number of reasons, it was considered impossible to successfully attack a certain distribution channel: some previous events were rooted in the minds of sales managers, suggesting that channel wouldn't be receptive to our products. This mentality was reverberated to area managers and to reps.

Most frequently used excuses ranged from poor after sale service to price positioning, from mtbf (mean time before failure, a measure of the reliability and durability of a product) to stock availability. Personally, knowing the business squeezed by our competitors in that particular channel, I never fully agree about these reasons, anyway recognizing some weaknesses from our side in technical area. At a certain point I decided to test the alibis: the channel was enucleated from the sales team, and I personally took charge of selecting a young rep, enthusiastic, proactive, optimistic and, above all, free from any conditioning.

I directly followed this guy, during the early stages of his new activity, assigning him an area within a fairly good purchase potential. After some induction training (company, products, market, style of selling) the guy started to operate. No contacts of any type with the rest of the team were allowed (that time, no cell phones existed!) To the surprise of the sales managers (and, I think, also with some disappointment) some contracts began to come in. Not so many, but enough to prove that thing could be done. After a while, orders increased a bit, and so segregation of this young rep came to an end. He was indeed invited to show his methods to incredulous colleagues. The end of the story showed that channel manned by five people, four of which belonged to the old team; sales results were, more or less, on line with the rest of the company.

What most people experience during their lifetime comes from the belief system deeply rooted within unconscious mind, in that continuum below threshold of consciousness, nevertheless housing the most important share of potential of every human being. Beliefs determine every moment of life of individuals and guide their thoughts, words, decisions, acts. What an individual believes influences his perceptions and his physiology. Beliefs create reality and are filters through which the objective facts of life and work take on different connotations and meanings for each person.

Since old ages, flashes of timeless wisdom argued that beliefs are a veil through which the reality is completely transformed; today, atomic physics theories and the latest neurosciences' discoveries state that the individual is the architect of his own reality, and has the power to change it. In Western world passing away of a loved one is felt as a tragic event, which generates extreme sadness and long lasting sorrow. Tears, longing, emptiness, sadness, black clothing are elements that pop up. Viceversa, in some Eastern cultures, death of a friend or a family member calls for happy parties, with singing, dancing, fun, colorful clothes and so much joy. This is because local beliefs assert the person migrate in an state in which he/she will live in extreme happiness, and therefore relatives rejoice for the bliss of their loved one. Sadness is even considered a form of selfishness.

This example is emblematic of the fact that a belief, by filtering the events that daily life brings with it, is often the absolute and final judge of what individuals feel, think, decide, behave, obtain.

Beliefs are created through a holistic process, ranging from genetic inheritance, local culture, emotions faced. So, beliefs sources are manifold:

• Genetic (coming from the genes of the ancestors), for example the fight-flight reflex.

• Experiential (those related to events with strong emotional content), for example, a child who touches a hot stove.

• Examples provided by parents, teachers, bosses, peers, friends.

• Ideas induced by the local culture (e.g. inculcated by the local dominant religion).

As a further example, if a teacher continuously repeats to a child he is stupid, it is likely the child validate that, and unconsciously limit his performance. If a boss insistently repeats to a rep that his results are the poorest of the department, it is likely that in the long run the rep, validating these words, unconsciously engage in self-limiting attitudes and produce results far below his possibilities. Obviously, also the opposite is true, providing to stay in an area of reasonableness (praise, congratulations, encouragements must be specific and sincere, to produce empowering beliefs).

A strong emotion that accompanies the event giving rise to a certain belief, helps a lot to save it. A strong emotion operates in both senses, to create an empowering belief, as well as a self-sabotaging one. In fact, intense emotions show an amplifying effect in regard to belief generation: negative emotions (fear, shame, hatred) in creating self-sabotaging beliefs, positive ones (love, happiness, satisfaction) in generating empowering ones.

However, these unconscious dynamics that sometimes represent a real challenge to common sense (and yet are strict rules like law of gravity) can create a belief only if the individual agrees and validates it. Nothing can turn into a belief, unless individual agrees with the message. This fact opens the door to a great opportunity: if belief needs an agreement from individual (at least those beliefs coming from life facts) we can say with certainty the power and responsibility of own beliefs are firmly in hands of person himself.

At the same time, another important question remains open: how one can identify self-sabotaging beliefs? This is obviously part of knowledge that people have of themselves, however the major issue is that most beliefs are unconscious: over time, have been accepted without being challenged. There are various techniques to locate limiting beliefs. Making use of psychological tests, going to therapy, or deeply meditating are three of many possible solutions. On the other side, there is a shortcut that can predict with good accuracy which are self-defeating beliefs. It's so simple that, often, individuals don't even consider it and, even in the face of clear facts, this shortcut is not widely accepted.

Look around you: whenever you see a repetition of specific negative results, you can be almost sure that there is an underlying self-sabotaging belief at work. If an athlete is constantly being defeated in a specialty (excelling in others), a wife always quarrels with her husband on certain topic, a student gets constantly negative results in specific exam, a salesman has a high dropout rate from his customers, you can be certain in that area there is a belief subtly working. A repetitive issue normally signals the presence of an underlying limiting belief.

Once found, it is advisable to challenge and to eradicate it. The abandonment of unwanted behaviors, in place for a long time, requires precise, systematic, determined actions. However, frequently, actions itself are not enough to kill the belief, since it became sclerotic and firmly accepted as true by the unconscious mind. Changing beliefs, behaviors and, therefore, results is much more than a conscious effort: it involves powerful forces, and needs to dismantle the barrier that the unconscious raises to protect its beliefs.

Kill and replace a belief requires much more than a simple act of will; requires that person change something at a very deep level. Also, what should be changed to get best results, may not be obvious. Reason which surfaces, looking like the issue, might not be it, since it represents only the effect, not the cause.

Most salesman still unable to get the results they want to achieve are probably hostage of most popular beliefs about market and themselves; what they have agreed to believe conditions them completely! All usual sales training / coaching activities related to the increase of their sales skills (especially if courses and coaching are updated and advanced) are certainly a good help; however, if rep does not critically analyze his behavior, strength and pervasiveness of their eventual self-sabotaging beliefs are capable of undermining the foundations of any attempt to improve. You can change your results, changing way of thinking: thinking changes decision, decision will change action, action changes the result. Apparently, the process seems simple, but if it did, the world would be populated only by sales superstars, and all we know this isn't the case. One must not only understand what to change, but also how to change it. This text seeks to reveal the true nature of what many salesmen believe and practice and proves, once and for all, how to replace the old self-sabotaging beliefs with new and highly productive ones.

Some time ago, the title of a sales manual intrigued me, and I bought the book. In an early chapter, the author asked the reader what was the issue that was preventing reader himself to achieve desired sales performances. A question aiming to generate awareness and stimulate solutions. Surely an important question. Indeed, a formidable question. Too bad it was a wrong question.

Answer is: "Nothing." There's nothing preventing any salesman to get results he "would like" to get. Every rep gets what is urged to obtain from his belief system (the unconscious goals his beliefs have defined). What we strongly want at a subconscious level is represented by our own beliefs about ourselves, our job, our market, our competition, our results and our potential. To pursue these goals unconscious mind uses that 95% of computing power lying below the consciousness threshold. The remaining 5% is available to conscious mind and, although directed to other goals, succumbs to the critical mass, to the power of impact of higher part of individual's potential.

The first step is to improve awareness. To make any changes you need to know what to change, you have to go to the heart of the problem, you have to act surgically, addressing real cause of issue. Therefore, salespeople who want to change for the better their results, have to act at core beliefs level: identifying hindering beliefs, removing them, and replacing them with more helpful ones. Adopting empowering thought patterns provides unconscious effective instructions that allow the mind to guide the individual right where he wants to go. This "autopilot" is able to overcome obstacles, to create facilitating conditions, to generate motivation, not letting anything distracting energies and skills from the real goals.

6 - SELF ESTEEM

Educators, parents, psychologists, politicians and business leaders agree on the need to develop a high self-esteem in individuals. Acceptance of self and others, optimism, determination, clear vision of own goals, tolerance for risk and ambiguity, clarity about weaknesses and strengths, resilience, are surefire keys to succeed, despite inevitable hassles. All those attributes are typical of people with high self-esteem. Conversely, doubts about own abilities, feelings of inadequacy, fear of failure, uncertainty, frequent changes of desires and goals, hesitation, procrastination, are all symptoms that denote a lack of self-esteem.

One of the difficulties that researchers are facing, in precisely define the concept of self-esteem, is that this attribute has been approached over the years, from many points of view. In some cases it has been perceived as a psychodynamic process, in others (from point of view of most part of cognitive and behavioral lines of thoughts) as a model to reproduce. Further, in other cases (from an experiential perspective) in terms of attitudes. Since the self-esteem has objectively both sociological and psychological attributes, achieving a single definition has been rather complex.

All in all, experts generally agree that self-esteem includes cognitive, emotional and behavioral elements. Cognitive elements relate to the fact that individual consciously assess any discrepancies between ideal self, the person he would like to be / become and a realistic perception, here and now, of himself. Emotional element refers to the emotions that arise in the individual, considering these discrepancies. Finally, behavioral aspect is manifested through assertiveness, resilience, decisiveness, benevolence, respect for himself and others.

In addition to that, generally self-esteem manifests a fluctuating magnitude, depending from external events (and their perceived consequences) that impact on person. In this light, self esteem can also be defined as situational.

For english vocabulary the definition of self-esteem is "the evaluation of self, which expresses the extent to which a person consider himself capable, important and of value"; in psychology, as already mentioned, it is considered to be the way you see yourself and represents the degree of confidence in values, abilities and in importance of yourself. On the whole, these two concepts coincide enough.

From both of them we can see something of great importance: evaluation of self and way of seeing oneself are two definitions that imply that self-esteem is something subjective, therefore not corresponding to an absolute "score" but , being the result of an evaluation (often linked to elements entirely subjective and changeable over time), it is simply the idea that a given person has created about himself at a given time. So, being self-esteem subjective, if it does not fully meet expectations, it can be changed!

In fact, self-esteem is one of those core beliefs unconsciously affect decisions, behaviors and results of people. Changing your self-esteem leads you to change the signals sent to your nervous system and to outside world. The change in these signals changes your actions and your results. However, usually self-esteem (and its daughter, self-confidence) are quite often rooted in the belief system of each of us, so changing them is something challenging.

An authoritative definition of self-esteem

Dr. Nathaniel Branden, one of the best-known American psychotherapists, the precursor of a series of studies on self-esteem, defined it as "the ability to perceive himself as a competent individual , able to successfully address the challenges of life, and worthy to receive well-being and happiness." Subsequently, Dr. Christopher Mruk, professor of psychology at Bowling Green University, said that this definition has successfully passed the test of time in terms of accuracy and truthfulness.

This idea of self-esteem is deeply connected with a sense of completeness and value of own lives; this value is sometimes confused with a simple positive feeling about themselves, when it is proven that should embody a high degree of satisfaction and contentment, more tied to basic human values.

The worth of this definition lies in the fact it is useful in making the distinction between an authentic self-esteem and another one, just superficial. A sense of personal value without the possession of social skills is just as limiting as the presence of social skills without a sense of value.

Moreover, the feeling of a strong value prevents self-esteem to slip out to arrogance, since it is able to keep the individual focused on ethical models; at the same time, the awareness of own skills does not result in narcissism, since high self-esteem values are counterbalanced by as much value for other people. Therefore, behavioral patterns defined as egotistical, selfish, self-referential, tending to boast and bullying can often denote defensive attitudes, typical of the lack of self-esteem. One final thought on the question is whether it is possible or not that self-esteem could be possessed in an excessive amount. The answer is no, as a good self-esteem is like a good health: one cannot have too much of it.

Self-esteem and social life

Although it is difficult to correlate the lack of self-esteem with the most common social problems, from a clinical standpoint links were proven between low self-esteem and problems such as violence, harmful substance abuse or too much food, school dropouts, business failures. Therefore, although it is hard to prove that a low self-esteem could always be the cause of such abnormal behavior, researchers reached the certainty that it is a major cause for which certain individuals highlight such disorders. Conversely, the same researchers, analyzing the profiles of people active, vital, optimistic, determined, who have achieved success, have always found the presence of a high degree of self-esteem.

Self-esteem and self-confidence are very important at every stage of life. Unfortunately, many people do not possess the appropriate extent of self esteem. When this happens, it creates a vicious circle: the lack of self-esteem generates behaviors consistent with "I can't do it" thoughts (indecision, vacillation, procrastination, lack of confidence, sadness, lack of enthusiasm, waiver) which sabotage success achievement. This in turn generates, in the person that fails, a further decrease of self-esteem, which produces more negative results. Viceversa, a good degree of self-esteem triggers behaviors consistent with "I can do it" thoughts (enthusiasm, energy, decision, happiness, confidence, perseverance) that facilitates the achievement of the set goals. This, in turn, strengthens self-esteem.

Self-esteem is the difference between feeling unstoppable and, conversely, feeling at the mercy of negative life events. The perception that an individual holds of himself possesses a huge impact in forming the impression of others about him. In fact, the success of any individual is not as much dependent from what people think about him, but from what he thinks about himself.

How self-esteem manifests itself

The level of self-esteem shows up in many ways: throughs, behavior, body language, speech.
Therefore, the person with high self-esteem communicates with great effectiveness (even if unconsciously) a clear message about him, a message of authoritativeness, power, consistency, success. Obviously, since often any given behavior calls for the same one, the other person probably (also unconsciously) will answer an acceptance message and will put himself on the same wavelength. Conversely, a person with low self-esteem uses a communication model that carries messages of insecurity, hesitation, incoherence, fragility, pushing the other party, in this case, to respond with refusal behaviors.
In the table below some thoughts and behaviors are shown, which typical of the two opposite polarities.

High self-esteem	Low self-esteem
Doing what seems right, even in presence of criticism from other people	Govern own behavior in accordance with other people's ideas
Be willing to take a reasonable risk and enduring actions until the goal is hit	Staying within own comfort zone, fearing failure
Admit mistakes and learn from them	Working hard to hide own mistakes in the eyes of others, and hope to resolve

	them before someone spots them
Awaiting quietly that someone congratulates for a well done task	Boost own skills to as many people as possible
Graciously accept any congratulation: "Thank you, I worked hard on this project, and I am glad you appreciate it"	Refuse definitely any congratulation: "Oh, this project was an easy task and anybody else could have done it even better"

If in everyday life self-esteem is important, in sales it even becomes a critical success factor. The fact that a salesman is not able to send positive messages to his buyer, could irretrievably jeopardize his influencing skills, simply because it shows misalignment between conscious and unconscious mind. This dystonia in the message greatly dampens the effectiveness of any sales action, often producing discouraging results.

What to do to raise self-esteem

In addition to what has been written in the beliefs chapter, there are a number of effective tips to raise self-esteem. Those who decide to adopt following tips, can greatly benefit from them. *Dress well and take care of your body:* even if one cannot judge a book from its cover, certainly clothing and care of themselves affect the self- perception of the individual, and that of others. Dressing sloppy, messy, dirty (although sometimes imperceptibly) affects the idea that a person makes about himself, and the way they interact with others. Not mentioning the image others make about him. The opposite occurs, when the individual dress carefully and with a bit of refinement. This does not mean you have to spend a fortune in clothes and cosmetics. A golden rule is "spend twice and buy half". Instead of buying many cheap clothes, you should buy less things, but with higher quality. Incidentally, in the long term you'll save money because high quality usually has a longer life.

Walk with decision: One of the typical elements to (sketchily) evaluate an individual is to observe his walk. Is it slow? Tired? Suffering? Or it is energetic, brisk, with long steps? As a general rule, a high self-esteem is coupled with a brisk walk. This shows the individual has commitment, places to go, important things to do. One can increase self-esteem and self-confidence by putting a little bit of pepper in his own walk. An increase of 25% in the step speed helps also in feeling better.

Adopt a good posture: As for the walk, the postures an individual usually takes are very revealing. Individuals with sloping shoulders and lethargic movements could demonstrate a low level of self-esteem and self-confidence. You probably are not thrilled to have relations with themselves and do not consider them so important. Conversely, firm and upright posture suggest opposing considerations. Taking erected and open positions (eye contact, vertical spine, slightly prominent chest, legs slightly apart if you stand still, or slightly longer steps if you are walking) automatically help you generate a higher self-esteem and self-confidence. In addition, other people get a better feeling about you.

Make a commercial about yourself: One of the best ways to learn how to build trust is to attend a course on how to arrange a self motivational speech. Unfortunately, such opportunities are rather uncommon. You can get almost the same effect by creating a sort of commercial about you. Write a motivating speech of 30-60 seconds that emphasizes your strengths and the results you've achieved, then say it loud in front of the mirror, every time you want to raise your self-esteem.

Exert gratitude: When we focus too much on what we want, often the mind creates reasons why these desires can not be fulfilled. This leads to dwell on own weaknesses. One of the best ways to avoid that is exerting gratitude. Spend a few minutes a day to mentally listing everything you've got, and be grateful. Remember your successes, your skills, your good times, your health, your wealth, and give thanks for that (to yourself, your parents, god, fortune, destiny). You'll be surprised about how much this will help to raise your self-esteem; you will also find further strength to continue on your journey.

Praise others: when an individual thinks negatively about himself, often projects that perception also to those around him, in the form of malignancy or gossip. To break this vicious cycle get the habit of praising others, for all the good that they have done or are doing. By doing so you will become well-liked and this will increase your self-esteem. Furthermore, searching for the good in others will increase your ability to find the good in yourself.

Sit in the front row: Often in schools, conferences, assemblies, people tend to sit in the back side of the room. Many people prefer a rear row as they wish to avoid being noticed. This sometimes reflects a lack of self-esteem. By deciding to sit in the front row, you kill this irrational fear and build self-esteem and self-confidence. You will also more visible to the Vip people involved as teachers or speakers.

Speak: Sometimes, during group discussions, some people remain silent, fearing their arguments might be judged foolish or not so relevant. This fear is not justified: usually people are more oriented to benevolence rather than malevolence. Making an effort to speak in every group discussion, improves your speech and you become more confident. All this contributes to self-esteem.

Do some gym: Fitness has an important impact on the level of self-esteem. Who's out of shape more often than not feels insecure and potentially rejected, and lives with a lower energy level. Conversely, some physical activity improves the appearance, deliver more energy, and allows you to better perform your duties. Fitness not only makes you feel better physically, it also creates a better psychological image of yourself.

Help others: Often people find themselves trapped inside their own desires. They focus too much on themselves and too little on the needs of others. If they stop thinking too much to themselves, while focusing on how they can contribute to the wealth of others, they will cease worrying about their own weaknesses. The more you contribute to the general welfare, the more you are rewarded for that, and this generates sharp increases in your self-esteem level.

Avoid to make comparisons: A low level of self-esteem can also coming by an environment that places too much emphasis on success and personal achievement, according to parameters that can sometimes be quite arbitrary (career, wealth, material possessions). In fact, each person is different from all others, and possesses unique attributes; each individual is a prototype. On this basis, you can strengthen your self-confidence and avoid comparing yourself with other individuals (who may, apparently, appearing as persons of greater caliber); instead emphasize your strengths and your successes.

Smile often: Try to smile and, simultaneously, to have pessimistic thoughts. You'll find that you can not, if the smile is sincere. The conscious mind can only focus on a few items at a time, and the smile monopolizes these attention units, taking resources from other emotions. Besides, who smiles often literally lives in a better biochemical environment than those who rarely smile, as the gaiety free neuropeptides that further elevate the level of well-being. In turn, this has a positive effect on self-esteem and self-confidence.

Focus on your strengths: Often repeat to yourself all your positive qualities, the successes you've got, the rewards you have won. This helps to focus your attention on everything important and positive you have been able to win, and raises quite a lot your self-esteem.

Do not take criticism as a personal attack: Never give anyone a chance to feel good making you feel bad. Low self-esteem is, unfortunately, infectious. Cultivate an objective view of the facts, and instead disassociate yourself from any problems that you or someone else might think you have created.

Learn from your mistakes: Often, in what people do (especially with regard to the sale) not everything always goes your way. A wrong client, a wrong decision, a ruined relationship, a customer lost. In all these cases, the most common attitude is that of blaming himself, looking for a scapegoating, making a self-accusation. Instead, find the good which almost always could sleep in any event, and use it to your advantage. It will be a great help in raising your self-esteem level. In fact, what is called "mistake" is simply a necessary step towards learning, a very valuable information on what to avoid, because it's proven it does not produce the expected results. Especially in sales, it is frequently to trigger vicious circles, from completely random facts.

A rep makes a few calls during which, for various reasons, does not sell; so he begins to focus on a series of pessimistic thoughts that eat away his self-confidence. "I am no longer able to convince customers, the market is now too difficult for me, competition is crushing me, I have become too soft in negotiations." All this has a bad effect on his self-esteem, and his performance begins to decline. New accusations to himself, again a downward self-esteem, and so on. Viceversa, an effective approach starts from cold and sincere analysis of the reasons why orders have not been secured (the client is illiquid, the product is new and not yet tested enough, my competitor X was quicker than me, this time I have not been effective in closing at the right moment). The next move is to re-check the situation, with enthusiasm and determination to successfully conclude the sale later.

The fear of failure

At this point, I feel the need to devote a few words to one of the most frequent salespeople's issues, directly connected with the lack of self-esteem: the so-called fear of failure. Western society has placed so much emphasis on material success, that the so-called failure had become a term that generates high repulsion level. The failure is definitely a bitter pill to swallow, but each person must fail at some point of their life, to learn something new.

The important thing is not the fact that the individual has failed, but the way in which he accepted and metabolized that failure. An individual can allow himself to feel destroyed by the failure, or force him to use it to strengthen his skills and determination to achieve higher goals at future times. Who fears failure should remember that the most successful people in the world have often had to fail many times, in the course of their life, to gain extraordinary successes. However, what made the difference was their willingness to learn from mistakes and use these informations as a learning process, to finally hit their goals.

The fear of failure creates anxiety, and magnifies any problem. A salesman with the fear of failure can become too competitive or worse, aggressive, as he starts to see every customer as a potential trap. This subtracts positive emotions to an activity which, in itself (at least for those who loves it) is joyful and fun. Moreover, the fear of failure makes nervous and anxious the salesman, and becomes an hurdle for high performances, making erratic and animated by a low energy level any salesman.

To win this strongly self-limiting behavior, the first step is to accept own imperfections. Nobody is perfect and any person, who loves herself and others, should tolerate falls on occasion, and should use them as a springboard for the next time. In all cases, always remember that the failure of today is often the success of tomorrow.

Excess of self-esteem

For salespeople, there is another trap for their performances, this time related to a matter that could be partly explained by an excess of self-esteem, a not quite balanced behavior: egotism. Technically it is defined as "to assign too much importance to themselves and to own life experiences". It's connected with vanity and selfishness. It's very detrimental to the sales activities, as a classic "by-product" of egotism is represented by low listening skills. The egotism has roots on the belief that those affected by it are better than others.

Actually the concepts of inferiority and superiority represent a dichotomy created by humans. In addition, the constant criticism (which sometimes comes from narcissistic attitudes) is a major cause of disagreement between people. There are some signs that one is suffering from egotism, and among them what follows.

• Think about the beggars as inferior beings, rather than as individuals in need of love;

• Having a vocabulary peppered with "me" and "I";

• Thinking always and only to own advantages;

• Thinking others' losses are own gains.

All this also results in low social attitudes, able to turn into real killers of any positive sales result. What then, if you believe you have an egotist attitude? A good idea is to work on yourself, focusing on how you can contribute to the welfare of others even before your own one.

Self-esteem frequent asked questions

What are the main indicators showing a high degree of self-esteem?

•   Possession of a chronic good mood

•   Being happy and peaceful for most of the time. Moodiness is rare.

•   Laughing often, and holding a belief system supporting positive behavior

- A lot of available energy, and the ability to complete most of your tasks

- Showing friendship, and a pleasure in staying with other people

- Ability to attract and fascinate others

- Habit of watching others in the eyes

- Being able to take some risks, and being independent and autonomous

• The behaviors acted out by a person with high self-esteem, and that in turn influence the attitudes of others, include: positive dialogue with themselves, consistency and clarity, keeping promises, gratitude for being who you are, ability to forgive, empathy, compassion and ethical values.

Self-esteem is a prerogative of a few, or anybody can develop it?

Anyone with an average IQ can develop self-esteem up to a very high degree. This route is facilitated by parents, teachers, co-workers, bosses, friends and peers. Sometimes, in the presence of a still unresolved trauma, it becomes difficult to access to high levels of self-esteem. However, whatever the initial conditions are, one can still improve it.

Self-esteem means feeling good about themselves?

Self-esteem goes far beyond that. It's a particular way of perceiving the self and involves various criteria: evaluative, emotional and cognitive. Requires a careful behavior: moving toward what you want instead of getting away from what you fear, treat facts with respect rather than remove them, operate on the basis of personal responsibility instead of blaming others. And living as people able to cope with the traditional life challenges, having the confidence to be able to make appropriate choices, responding proactively to change, and having the belief that success, satisfaction, well-being and joy are a natural and possible condition for everybody.

Focusing too much on self-esteem encourages self-centering attitudes?

Rationally, we should focus on self-esteem just for the pleasure of the act itself; it would be better to focus on those activities that allow it grow and develop, as habit of living in the here and now, acceptance of self, assertiveness, empowerment, energy in pursuing own goals, resilience in the face of obstacles, research of integrity and consistency. Self-esteem requires a strong orientation to reality, and is rooted in a great respect for the facts and the truth. An excessive self-centering attitude is often a symptom of a low self-esteem. If we are sure about something, we don't need to continuously underline it, with behaviors ranging from exerting pressure, being disrespectful of others, or even arrogant: we simply live it in our daily life.

It is possible to have a too high self-esteem?

It seems that it isn't, especially when it comes to fact-based self-esteem. You can not enjoy too much self-esteem as you can't enjoy too much good health: you are completely healthy, and that's it. However, sometimes, when people lack self-esteem will become arrogant, overly proud, screaming, as a compensatory mechanism. Often, their issue is not having a too big ego, but rather the opposite.

Which aspects influence self-esteem?

There are many factors at play. Certainly parents are one of the most important ones; they may facilitate or hinder the acquisition of an healthy self-esteem. However, they do not have the possibility to determine the level of self-esteem of their children. Each event experienced coming from social context has the power to build or dismantle self-esteem. In all this we have to remember the role that the individual himself plays, through the daily choices selection and decisions making process. We aren't the public, we are the actors of the show, and we have direct responsibility for what happens to us.

Is self-esteem the result of the approval from important people?

The answer is no. If we lived in a non-responsibility regime, without consistency, without clear goals and the strength to pursue them, perhaps self-esteem would be proportional to the approval obtained from other influential, important or powerful people. When people betray themselves and their own ideals, to gain approval, experience a jolt to their self-esteem. What benefits could give us gaining world's approval, while at the same time our one is lost? It's well known the fact that, often, kids try to gain peers' approval, especially when peers are considered influential or dominant. This directly influences kids' self-esteem. However, one should consider that this kind of self-esteem is very fragile, and usually collapses when, for whatever reason, the hard-earned approval would be withdrawn or denied.

Possession of luxurious items, popularity and material well-being automatically leads to high self-esteem?

Sometimes those who lack self-esteem are convinced the answer is yes, but the truth is that in the world there are people who have achieved fame, wealth, possess charming objects, are followed by thousands (if not million) fans, and yet feel empty inside. These individuals, as a compensation strategy for a life subtly and unconsciously dedicated to anxiety and depression, often are not able to spend an entire day without taking harmful substances. Fame, wealth, beauty, success does not guarantee anything, if they are not naturally supported by self-esteem. In such cases, the lack of it often makes people feel like "impostors", fearing to be "discovered" and lose all benefits.

Praising and encouraging appropriate behaviors helps self-esteem growing?

This depends on what you mean by "praising" and "encouraging". If we talk about a child who is acting consciously and responsibly, whose behavior is praised and encouraged, the answer is yes. Moreover, in such a case, we can assume that such behavior will be reinforced. If the virtuous behavior patterns get ignored, ridiculed and punished it is likely that the child does not repeat it. In both cases, his self-esteem can be affected.

However, to be truly effective, praise (or rather, recognition) must be based on objective reality (and therefore should not be extravagant or exaggerated) and addressing the behavior rather than the character. Use of phrases like "you're an angel", "you're always so good," or "you are very pretty and lovable" can generate anxiety, because the child knows that in many cases this is not true. Rather, phrases like "you have done a good job" seems safer.

Praise, encouragement and recognition should be carefully weighed, to avoid creating addiction from the approval of others. The objective is to ensure that the child himself becomes his own source of approval, rather than feel dependent on others for being praised. Therefore it is necessary to avoid to bomb the child with continuous feedback.

It's true that nothing is able to worry those who are endowed with high self-esteem?

Some self-esteem enthusiasts believe that it solves all problems of existence. This probably isn't completely true: for instance, fight is a fundamental component of life. Sooner or later people experience anxiety and pain, and while self-esteem can make them much less susceptible to life excesses, it is not able to completely vaccinate. We should think of self-esteem as something like the immune system, which is not able to completely preserve the body from diseases, but it decreases their number and severity.

A high level of self-esteem, if achieved, lasts forever?

Any value pertaining to life requires continuous maintenance to be preserved. If we do not continue to breath fresh air, we are not able to stay alive. The same principle applies to self-esteem: if you reach a good level of self-esteem, you have to make maintenance to it to preserve it. Nothing, not even the self-esteem, can be kept alive and healthy without any maintenance.

What comes first, self-esteem or success?

A lot of studies make evidence that the individual should be equipped with a good level of self-esteem to have the strength to endure long enough to be able to achieve success. These studies suggest that success is the symptom, and not the cause, of a good self-esteem. In all ways, success certainly reinforces self-esteem, therefore both aspects are intimately linked. The question could be put in different terms: how to act so that the increase in the level of self-esteem and success are achieved at the same time? The answer to this question is in the last part of this book.

Reflections through celebrities

To conclude this chapter, here is some food for thought, about how some people have been able to persevere until success, despite failures they have encountered in the course of their lives, and how to achieve their goals has been supported by a unshakable self-esteem.

• Albert Einstein, in 1895, was rejected from qualifying exams of the ETH in Zurich. Moreover, he learned to speak only at three years old and reading after seven.

• Al Neuhart began working, still a kid, as collector of excrements; during adulthood he founded the largest newspaper in the United States (USA Today).

• Lev Tolstoy was called "unable and unwilling to learn" by his teachers, and retired early from the university.

• Walt Disney was fired by his employer for lack of ideas, and also went bankrupt several times before he built Disneyland.

• Fred Astaire, in 1933, got an audition from MGM, which cut short him with an harsh judgment on his skills as a dancer.

• Johnny Weissmuller, who suffered from a severe form of polio as a child, was convinced that he could become a champion in swimming. Despite the disease that had plagued him, not only won five Olympic gold medals and 52 US national titles, but also established 64 world records, and became the most famous Tarzan of the movies.

• Many publishers refused the short story about a seagull flying high in the sky, Jonathan Livingston Seagull, before McMillan decided to publish it, in 1970. In 1975, after seven million copies sold in the US alone its author, Richard Bach, was considered one of the best known writers of the twentieth century.

7 - HOW ALL ABOVE SHOWS UP

When you are in front of other individuals, you communicate. Communication occurs whether you speak, or stay silent. Indeed, sometimes the silence is an even more explicit and eloquent message. The process of communication between individuals is mostly done through kind of words (verbal language), through rhythm, tone, speed, breaks of words (para-verbal language), through gestures, facial expressions, posture, limb movements, behavior (body language). These three elements combine together and, with different weights, create the so-called communication process.

A study of 1967 of the Armenian psychologist Albert Mehrabian found that verbal language helps to qualify the message up to 7%, the para-verbal language up to 38%, and the body language up to 55%. So, according to this study, only 7% of the information content of a given topic is verbally given, 38% goes through vocal elements, and the most important part (55%) is entrusted to the facial expressions, head, arms, hands, torso, legs, feet movements, and other micro-behaviors. Therefore, if words were missed, would remain another 93% of informative content, sent from a source to one or more receivers. The study obviously refers to face to face communication.

So. the "how", for the purposes of understanding the message sent, has at least many times as much the value of the "what". In reality, these percentages may vary, depending on the particular scenario, but not substantially. Mehrabian himself told clearly that these figures are typical of a scenario where a source communicates an emotion-dense message to a receiver. If the topic, let's say, isn't emotional but technical, those percentages might be different, but not that much.

Each of these three components of the message has conscious and unconscious contents. For example, the choice of words is in principle controlled by the conscious mind; however, experiencing intense emotions, a part of the choice of words is unconscious, and follows emotions. Para-verbal part is mainly managed by the unconscious mind; however, there may be cases (e.g. an expert lecturer) in which the conscious mind exerts a certain control. Finally, the body language is largely entrusted to the unconscious mind. So, in the process of communicating, we can say with a good approximation that the conscious mind controls 10, maybe 15% of the message, while the rest is more or less committed to the unconscious mind.

This means that core beliefs, self-esteem, emotional intelligence govern the part of the message far more important. Translated into a sales pitch, this means that a salesman does not communicate what he wants, but what he really thinks. About himself, about his product, his company, his competitors, the market, the customer in front of him.

Sale is a process where emotion plays an important role; so it is almost impossible to exert a close control on the content of the communication process. The fact is that both parts (vendor and buyer) line up on the field four entities: two conscious and two unconscious minds. All them interact at two levels at the same time. The conscious level focus on logic and reasoning, the unconscious on emotions, feelings, intuitions. Then, the four entities have to come up to a decision. All that is worsened by the current markets' shrinking, profit decreasing, and growing competition. It is a pretty much complicated story, isn't it? That's why the job of the sale is often considered damn hard.

How is a buyer reacting to a vendor who communicates, for example, to have a poor self-esteem? How is a buyer reacting to a rep that shows to feel nervous and at unease? How can a customer buy from a salesman that communicates to consider of no importance any point of view other than his own, or that manifests embarrassment stating the price, or showing impatience with the needs of the client?

The power of non-verbal behavior

The higher power of non-verbal compared to verbal, has many causes. Probably the biggest is that unconscious mind is much more powerful than conscious one, in controlling main elements of behavior (for consistency, let's repeat 95% vs. 5%). Another reason could be the fact that, in the course of a face to face communication, the body continuously sends signals, while the duration of the flow of words is short and fluctuating: you say something, than stay silent while listening to the answer, all interspersed with silences. A third reason might be that the facilitators of the movement and posture of our body are about 600 different muscles (only 90 in the face), absolutely impossible to simultaneously control. In addition there are many other related elements. Among them, the biochemical environment of the body (anxiety fill the blood with endorphins and accelerates the speed of speech; quietness decreases heart rate and relaxes the vocal cords). So the control of the message and the behavior mainly falls under the domain of the unconscious, which moves them according to its own rules. These rules are dictated primarily by core beliefs, emotions, feelings, no matter if they are apparently irrational.

The autenticity of the metacommunication

The part of the message beyond words (para-verbal and non verbal) is also called metacommunication. This term literally means communicating something about the communication itself. The most important consequence of this is related to the authenticity of the metacommunication, which expresses exactly what the individual thinks, without the usual social filters and logic convenience of the specific moment. Therefore, you can control it only by acting on its root causes. Any other attempt would be doomed to failure, because the conscious mind (volition) does not have the resources to manage the unconscious one.

Attempt to control the metacommunication, in order to align it with the spoken words generates, at best, a series of inconsistencies between the verbal and paraverbal / nonverbal plans, which are immediately recognized by receiver, rapidly lowering his level of credibility of message's sender. In a communication act, verbal part is called "content", while para-verbal and non-verbal is indicated as "relationship". In other words, message content is what words convey; all the rest (which is mainly physical behavior) shows the relationship between sender and content, between sender and receiver, and what sender thinks is the relation between content and receiver.

It looks complicated, doesn't it? In fact it is, unless you accept to split the message in two parts: the argument / the reason why, and the deep thoughts of the sender about the message itself, and its context. The voice of the unconscious mind speaks louder than anything else within message and, through certain behaviors, plainly shows which its thoughts are .

So, a rep sure to can get success, sure his product is good enough, convinced to be able to close the sale, motivated, resilient, who considers top notch the client's needs, will spontaneously adopt behaviors naturally aligned with the verbal content. This makes message open, consistent and authoritative. On the other side, other things being equal, another hesitant, doubtful, pessimistic salesman, who gives up easily at first hassle, will tend to show his weaknesses. Unconscious part of the message will tend to be hesitant, doubtful, pessimistic as well, no matter which words are used: unconscious mind will shout its deep thoughts, probably very different from sales pitch's words.

The components of the body which communicate

All body muscles are involved in metacommunication, so the relevant body part are the following.

- Head (eyes, mouth, tongue, teeth, eyebrows)

- Arms (fingers, hands, elbows, shoulders)

- Torso (neck, chest, stomach, belly, back)

- Legs (thighs, knees, ankles, feet)

Given that individual body signals sent from a single limb or a particular anatomical component (eyes, mouth, fingers), if considered alone, may not be fully representative of real emotions, mental state and deep thoughts of the individual, it is important to put any single behavior in a context. So, we have to consider entire behavioral patterns, generally able to describe the inner state in a rather clear way.

In addition, one of the secrets of an acceptable body language reading is to check all facts happening at the same time. For example, if in a given scenario an individual simultaneously crosses legs, arms, ceases eye contact and tends to move away with the torso, probably all these signals might be a sign of disappointment or / and disagreement. At the same time, only one of the above movements could have other causes (looking for a more convenient posture or a moment of distraction, due to fatigue). In all ways, certain fundamental signals often send quite unique messages.

Following some of the most common body signals will be discussed. You can easily realize what they are, among them, those that facilitate and those that hinder you. The latter, and the consequent behaviors, are probably a symptom of some self-sabotaging causes, which should be eliminated from your belief system and replaced with others, able to potentiate your sales action. If so, you will detect new signals emitted by your body, this time able to support more productive behaviors.

Head is considered one of the most genuine signals emitter (in fact, head is body part that receives greater part of attention from message's recipient). At same time it is a part that cannot be consciously controlled, just for its great motility and large amount of muscles that compose it (you can simulate a smile, but engaging only some of the many dozens of muscles in charge to form a sincere one, and therefore smiling in a patently artificial and forced fashion). Main signals from the head are the following.

• Head down: this is generally considered sign of submission or defense (gaze goes down, chin covers carotid); it can also be interpreted as sign of fatigue. An exception is represented by a downward movement, accomplished only once, for assent. This can be interpreted as sign of power or authority (just nod once, no need to repeat it).

• Head up: chin at normal height is generally interpreted as sign of listening and interest (eyes pointing towards speaking person). If position (and gaze) is higher more than needed, it could be sign of boredom, or experience's recall.

• Side tilting: if coupled with tight lips it can signal indecision, need for further clarification. A firm lateral tilt can also be sign of interest.

• Repeated vertical tilting: broadly interpreted as a sign of interest and, above all, consent. In the latter case it is often accompanied by grin. This movement, while listening, tends to encourage the speaker.

• Turning right and left: indicates almost always disagreement, and is a strong signal of denial

Mouth, as well, is broadly considered an important part for interpreting body language.

• Opening for breathing: inhale a large or fast breathe (usually, in the course of a normal sales pitch, you can breathe through your nose only) almost always indicates high level of anxiety (body needs more oxygen to prepare for fight or flight reaction).

• Breathing very wide (yawning) is strong sign of boredom, even more so if there is an ongoing attempt to repression of this act; frequent short inhalations may be signs of a strong pent-up sadness.

• Covering it by means of a hand: in Western cultures, social custom to avoid showing cavity of the mouth and block fumes or emissions of saliva; in other cases, hand covering can be linked to a desire to suppress a strong emotion (surprise, great sadness). In some cases (though you have to confirm this with presence of other signals) mouth is covered by issuer in event of lying.

- Upwards extremes: smile is usually an indicator of pleasure and contentment (should be confirmed by other signals of face and eyes, to make sure it is sincere). An half-smile (most often from left side) can indicate cynicism, sarcasm and uncertainty.
- Downward extremes: almost always indicate sadness, discouragement, frustration, anger.

Eyes are a key part of head, so are important in deciphering body language.

- Gaze downwards: often signals submission or guilt.
- Gaze upwards: it may be due to search for inspiration and to recall a memory, or highlight boredom (we try something more interesting on ceiling). Look at the top with head lowered usually indicates submission mixed with desire.
- Sidelong glances: in general can be interpreted as desire to move away from something negative, or (if it's a quick glance) internal thought or assessment of something. If it is long lasting can also signal irritation. The continuous movement from side to side may indicate a lie (unconsciously the person is looking for an escape route in case he was discovered), or conspiracy (ensures that no one else is listening).
- Slawing look from top to bottom of interlocutor's body more than one time can usually be considered a sign of superiority. It might also indicate an evaluation and "weighting" of interlocutor, to assess his potential danger, as enemy, or usefulness, as prey.
- Fleeting glances: usually a sign of desire (quick glances at a door or a window might signal desire to escape).

• Eye contact to interlocutor/partner is usually a sign of interest, especially if it is addressed to eyes of other. Eye contact for too long time can be experienced as inquisitorial; the breaking of eye contact by an interlocutor usually indicates disagreement, attempting to terminate dialogue, or perception of aggression.

• Quick glances from one eye to the other can be interpreted as a search for consensus. Sporadic eye contact usually signals insecurity and attempted manipulation, if not lie.

Upper limbs are considered just partially reliable because their conscious control presents a certain degree of ease (compared to legs and head); hands are one of the indicators most widely used, and should always be interpreted in conjunction with other signals.

•Cupped hands can be interpreted as care, protection, sense of fragility.

•Holding one hands with the other can indicate need of care (one gives himself self-care), or act of blocking them from doing something blameworthy, in case of anger or rage.

•Hiding one hand behind back (as well as keeping them motionless, clutching one another) may reveal an attempt to control them; so these signals may be indicators of attempted manipulation.

•Extending an object with both hands signals respect. It is typical from Eastern cultures, and often used in business relationships when a business card is handed over.

•Fiddling with objects is often a way to give vent to stress, anxiety and inner tension.

•Handshake: extending the hand with the palm up, usually indicates submission; attempt to dominate occurs when the hand is given with the palm down. Accompanying handshake with own left hand clutching right forearm of interlocutor boosts dominance signal. Strong and long lasting handshakes often shows an attempt to dominate, handshakes fast and weak look like an admission of subjection, or an attempt to retreat.

The way to move *torso and lower limbs*, as well as their position are considered important signals. In particular postures (both standing or sitting) provide important information about sender's mood. Legs and feet send powerful signals, as they are difficult to control. In case of conflict between signals of the upper and lower limbs, the latter are often the most reliable indicators.

Regarding posture, standing still, straight, with head held high, chest slightly prominent and legs slightly apart is generally regarded as an indicator of self-confidence and decision. Conversely, a stooped posture, with lowered head and neck drowned within shoulders, legs very close or even crossed is usually seen as a sign of insecurity, weakness, indecision, fear, shyness, feelings of inadequacy. The same applies for the walk: upright posture, with long and fast steps usually sends signals of self-confidence and self-esteem. Conversely, short and slow steps, bowed head, sagging shoulders are often interpreted as a lack of decision and self-confidence. In sitting positions, an upright posture in principle indicates attention and interest; sink into the chair could send signals of great relaxation and attention (however it should be confirmed with other signals).

Moving away from the other person, often means disinterest and denial. Sitting at the tip of the chair, in most cases, shows hurry, little interest, desire to leave. While seated, knees slightly apart for males are often interpreted as sign of relaxation and openness to the other party (the crotch is exposed); legged legs might mean a desire not to reveal himself. For ladies legs overlapping is much more frequent, and loses some importance, in terms of self-closure. For both sexes, twisted legs and ankles usually indicate poor desire to uncover themselves. Also for both sexes, toes heading towards an exit (door or window) often indicate a desire to escape (for lack of interest or fear). Finally, the frequent change of sitting position (as well as shaking a foot or leg) often signal nervousness, lack of interest, annoyance.

Lies and manipulation

During sales calls, sometimes, circumstances leave room for deceit and manipulation. Sometimes it happens that one party, in an attempt to hit its goals, try to lie and manipulate. Other times, it happens as a self-defense attitude, when the dominant feelings are insecurity and lack of confidence in own skills. In all cases, for salespeople, it is useful to be able to identify these signals, both to defend themselves from others, and to avoid to attack them.

When someone lies or intends to conceal his real thoughts and feelings, usually try to control himself and try to look spontaneous; unfortunately that allows some behaviors getting visible, especially if one ignores that a certain behavior could betray him. That's why observing body language can help detect lies. So, if someone tells fibs, a sudden twitch of the face, manipulating something, diverting the glance and other micro-behaviors are involuntary moves, letting true attitudes to pop up, and contradicting what one says. Although there is a belief that a lie is accompanied by certain instinctive actions (self-contacts, loss of eye contact, generalized nervousness) actually what transpires is just an emotion. So, even if one decides to lie, the more calm or detached he is , the more he can control himself. Conversely, the more he feels guilty or anxious, the less he can prevent signals indicating the presence of these emotions from escaping.

One of the most frequent actions, when one wants to hide a feeling, is a fake smile. As a lot of people might know, not all smiles are equal: from the analysis of facial expressions it is possible to identify over fifty different kind of smiles, each with own look and own special message.

By the mid-nineteenth century the French neurologist Duchenne de Boulogne had identified the characteristics of the sincere smile that involves, in addition to the muscles of the mouth, even those of the eyes. Generally, it has been noticed that people sometimes are fooled by fake smiles; the cause of these misunderstandings is the temporary inability (a conscious skill) to distinguish real smiles from fake ones. The common traits to genuine smile are the change in face appearance produced by the zygomatic major muscle contracting, at the same time raising the corners of the mouth up. The genuine smile is also characterized by a spontaneous contraction of a muscle of the eye, known as the pars lateralis, which creates the so-called "crow's feet" at the sides of the eyes. In addition, often, a slight lowering of the eyebrows, around the eyelids take place.

US scientist Paul Ekman, (teacher at University of Wisconsin), by measuring brain activity of various smiling people, has highlighted that only in the presence of contraction of pars lateralis muscle, brain regions that determine feelings of pleasure are activated. But when the smile is fake, "crow's feet" that are produced at the side of the eyes and the slight lowering of the eyebrows that appear in genuine smile are often absent. When used as a mask, the fake smile covers only the actions of the lower part of face. In addition, the fake smile is often asymmetric (more marked on the right side of the face, which is controlled by the left hemisphere) and characterized by an abnormal time of decay, so may appear and disappear way too fast compared to real one.

Also some variations of voice and manner of speaking may go neck and neck with lie or manipulation. A vocal trait distinguishing who is lying is tone which sounds shrill. If the person feels resentment, but want to hide it, his voice tends to become more metallic, dry and with higher volume. In this cases articulation of words is accelerated, words are often "eaten" and speech appears broken; furthermore, pauses between the words become shorter. If person is sad or unhappy (as in front of a disappointing gift) his vocal timbre results lower, weak and sighed. In this case, even talk is slowed down and pauses are longer.

Self-contacts are generally good companions of lies: often those who lie also tend to gesture less than usual. This is probably because they are more focused than usual on their words, and because reducing the gestures, feel less exposed to criticism.

One of things that those who lie do, is to manipulate objects, press something with fingers, fiddling with what is at hand, crumpling a piece of paper, shaking the pack of cigarettes, or pick up a pen or a phone like they were at the point to use it: however, in most part of cases, they remain unused. In such cases deception becomes sometime a pretext that allows to relieve the stress of a direct gaze, when it becomes unsustainable.

What motivates people to lie?

Us psychologist Robert Feldman cites self-esteem as one of the biggest culprits in our lying ways: "We find that as soon as people feel that their self-esteem is threatened, they immediately begin to lie at higher levels." Feldman believes many lies are simply for the purpose of maintaining social contacts by avoiding insults or discord. Small lies that avoid conflict are probably the most common sort of lie...and avoiding conflict is a top motivator for deception. For example: someone lying about traffic holding them up, rather than declaring it could say "oh, you look great in those pants" to achieve the effect of avoiding social conflict. This is a "make life easier" kind of lie.

In sales, sometimes salespeople use "partial lies", just to hidden something to their buyer, which could prevent them to buy. This phenomenon isn't considered a real lie, since it doesn't really deceive, but just partially hides some topics.

Back to the self-esteem angle, the farther one's true self is from its ideal self, the more likely people tend to lie to boost themselves up, in others' eyes or in their eyes... or perhaps in how they perceive others to perceive them. Clearly that is a hard train of thought to follow, but lying is a complex phenomenon.

How often do people lie?

One study, published in the Journal of Basic and Applied Psychology, found that 60 percent of people had lied at least once during a 10 minute conversation between two strangers. On average, subjects lied almost 3 times in a 10 minute conversation. Another study about 2000 Uk citizens claims men tell six lies a day, with women averaging 3 lies a day. The same research found most common lie (told by both sexes) being "Nothing wrong, I'm fine." In the United States, one study had 77 college students plus 70 community members keep a diary detailing their deceptions. The students admitted to lie an average of twice a day, while the community members lied about once per day.

As above mentioned, to truly understand others, body language must be globally seized and analyzed, especially when inconsistencies between verbal language and body language are detected. In fact, a dystonia is a strong indicator of an attempt (often unsuccessful) to self control, originated from the desire to manipulate the message sent out. In these cases, the perception of the listener is such that, often, gives rise to closures, which in turn generate further anxiety in the issuer, who tries to accentuate control, thereby further amplifying the differences.

The best thing to do is to be spontaneous, and attack the root causes that generate the symptoms. Whichever they are, spontaneity will create more consistency between three levels of communication process, will eliminates misalignment, and will booster credibility and authority of salespeople. In turn, that will become the best stepping stones to outstanding sales performance!

8 – MIND'S REPROGRAMMING IS POSSIBLE!

In computer language, programming is understood as set of activities that an individual (a programmer) roll out to teach a machine (a computer) to perform a specific task (communicate, do calculations and forecasts, edit a book, play music, cards or chess, or draw). Programming is required to provide instructions to machine in a language that it can easily understand and interpret, to allow it to use its computing power and be able to follow, without errors, given instructions.

At the same time, unconscious mind (a very powerful computer) can receive a set of instruction from a programmer (conscious mind) to perform certain tasks (in current case, following the scope of this book, selling better and with higher profits). Both "machines" share many similarities. Like a traditional pc, also the unconscious mind:

• Is multiprocessor (neurons function as processors, in a parallel architecture)

• Is wired (neuronal cells are connected each other by more than 160 Km of nerve fibers)

• Is equipped with an hard disk (the long-term memory)

• Is equipped with ram modules (the short-term memory)

• Is equipped with programs (beliefs, habits)

• Must accomplish some tasks (keeping alive the body that houses it and reaching certain goals)

• Needs energy to work (oxygen and glucose)

• Must be feeded by datas (from the sensory system).

"Bugs" in the programs

One of terms often used in informal IT language is "bug", which indicates an error (logic or syntactic) in a given set of instructions. This error prevents computer from performing certain tasks, or even force it to execute a task not desired by programmer. To eliminate these errors, one needs to analyze all instructions given to computer, locate the bug and correct it or, in most radical cases, completely reprogram the computer.

Even in unconscious mind there are bugs: we can regard them as disempowering beliefs and thought patterns unproductive of results, that do not allow the achievement of desired goals. They should be removed, to allow that 95% of computing power to properly carry out its tasks, and lead the individual where consciously he want to be led (again, following the scope of this book, selling better and with higher profits).

The reprogramming language of unconscious mind

Often what makes it impossible to unlock the resources of a given individual, giving him access to the highest performance, is the programming language consciously used, written with a logic and syntax the unconscious mind isn't familiar with. This often results in poor results, achieved with great efforts, indecision, procrastination, dissatisfaction. Contrary to what is commonly believed, volition only is not powerful enough to change a disempowering thought: volition is a conscious process that has little effect in the domain of the unconscious mind.

Using just volition, individual who wishes to change some deep aspects of himself, is likely to expose himself to feelings of powerlessness and frustration. This happens since he does not understand why, in the face of a very intense conscious desire, he doesn't succeed to change beliefs and, with them, his ways of reacting to a given situation and having productive behaviors.

Most suitable programming language for the unconscious mind consists of feelings (generated from stimuli coming from sensory system), emotions (anger, fear, sadness, joy, surprise, disgust, waiting, acceptance), images (the more vivid, the best). This means that, to change beliefs and thought, individuals must use emotions, feelings and images, rather than just words and linear thinking.

Since core beliefs control one's life in every sphere (relationships with others, self-esteem, self-image and self-confidence, decisions, behavior's effectiveness) following techniques to get rid of limiting beliefs are useful for all aspects of life, including sales. The methods here described are quite effective in improving:

- Core beliefs

- Self-Esteem

- Emotional Intelligence

As a result of these improvements, behaviors (including body language) change and start supporting success instead of failure. Of course, before starting any activity aiming at reprogramming the unconscious mind, it's of paramount importance identifying (with surgical precision) the area to which to intervene. This step is very important because makes thought/beliefs reorganization working faster and in a more effective way.

Talking about sales, the best advice that can be given to a salesman (whether already experienced, or novice) who wants to improve his results it is to analyze with great accuracy his performance, to realize what are the areas which needs to be modified. A task (establishing relationships, obtaining consensus, negotiation, needs' analysis, cold calls) recurrently producing bad results, is an almost certain indicator of need for action on the underlying belief. In addition, to identify potential improvement areas, it is useful to detect the presence of any reluctance to carry on any task typical of sales process (for example, reluctance to see new customers). These aversions are very likely signals of presence of underlying self-limiting beliefs.

At this point, a question arises: "What do I believe to experience this resistance?". The response, which might not come immediately, but only after few attempts, should provide an indication of what is the hassle to remove. Also, it can be useful to analyze the performance of salesmen to whom you want to look like, and identify the underlying beliefs that are supporting that results. These beliefs should be acquired. Likewise, the opposite analysis can be helpful: identify the beliefs that support those reps you don't want to look like. Realize whether these beliefs are also yours, or not; if yes, kill them.

How to eradicate a limiting belief, replacing it with an empowering one

Eradicate a limiting belief involves both conscious and unconscious mind; the first has the role of managing the process, from a point of view of volition and process; the latter is the subject of the process.

The first thing to do is locate a belief that is limiting your performance in a certain area. After that, in writing, you must execute following protocol: associate great pain to the limiting belief; weaken and undermine it; replace it with a new potentiating one; associate great pleasure to new belief; look for references about it; finally, live out and vividly visualize in advance its results. It's very important that this protocol is carried out in writing and then read aloud, rather than just mentally rehearsed. Using all senses will set in motion more powerful forces, favoring memory and sedimentation. So, take a sheet of paper, a pen, and then do as follows.

- Associate pain to the old limiting belief.

o How many opportunities you have already missed because of your limiting belief?

o What will be the emotional and economic cost of keeping that belief alive?

o What are the problems you, your family members, your relatives, your friends, your peers will face keeping the belief alive?

- Weaken and undermine it, with appropriate questions and seeking references which could cast doubt on its trueness.

o Am I sure that this is really so?

o Which are the elements that would confirm it, and are they really valid?

o Who might find absurd or ridiculous this belief, and why?

o Which are the sources it comes from, and are they completely trustworthy?

o What objective facts, if considered, can challenge it?

- Identify a new empowering belief, possibly in the same area of the old limiting one. For example, if you want to get rid of a belief that says: "I am unable to find new customers," the corresponding empowering belief might be: "I am so empathetic that search for new clients is easy for me."

▪ Find all possible references which confirm the new belief (things happened in the past, evidence/praises from third parties, real experiences, facts and figures of your personal/professional life, ...).

　　o What facts testify its truthfulness?

　　o How many times I had been able to do this?

　　o Who can confirm my skill?

▪ Associate great pleasure to your new belief.

　　o What will give me living with the new empowering belief?

　　o What will be the benefits for me and my loved ones?

　　o What emotional, financial and practical goals will I reach by living with this new belief?

▪ Live out and visualize the results your new belief will support you to get. Load the visualization with strong pleasure, ease, satisfaction feelings. The more real they will be, the more visualization process will work for you (more details on visualization techniques will follow).

Alpha state

The brain of the individual, in the course of 24 hours that make up a day, and carrying out all its activities, goes through a series of "operating states". Each of these states is associated with emission of electromagnetic waves, with different voltage and frequency. These states are:

• Waking state (Beta state)

• Deep relaxation and / or mild drowsiness state (Alpha state)

- Sleep state (Theta state)

- Very deep sleep state (Delta state)

In each of the four cases some features of the basic bioelectrical brain change, besides the fact that consciousness (typical of the waking state) diminishes until it completely disappears. Although there is no full agreement among specialists regarding the accuracy of the frequency of the different ranges of brain waves, which follows is a widely accepted compromise.

Wakefulness is the condition in which you find yourself during most daily activities (work, study, entertainment). That is, when you are focused on external stimuli; the frequency of the waves is around 20 cycles per second, and their voltage is 5 to 10 microvolts. Electromagnetic waves are emitted from the centers of conscious thought, which remains in control of the activity of the mind even if the eyelids are temporarily lowered. This state is called "Beta" and its waves have the same name.

The state of deep relaxation or mild drowsiness is typically achieved as a result of a deep relaxation of the muscles of the body, or in the presence of a very monotonous stimulus (auditory, tactile, visual). The frequency goes down around 8-12 cycles per second, and the voltage reaches 50 microvolts. In this condition the so-called day-consciousness begins to lose control of mind, and gives way to unconscious, and the individual is brought to lower eyelids. This condition is also called "Alpha" state, as are the respective electromagnetic waves. A sudden stimulus (light, noise) forces back the Beta state.

The Alpha condition is typical of the moments before sleep, or the first moments after waking; however it is a state which is accessed frequently during the daily activity. It can be provoked by watching a boring film or reading a particularly monotonous book, holding a very persevering thought, or making a total muscle relaxation. An even deeper relaxation leads brain in state of sleep (or "Theta") where external stimuli are no longer detected, unconscious takes hold of the mind and dominates the process.

At this stage dreams appear, the body sometimes shake, some words can be pronounced, but only stimuli that matter come from the unconscious. This is really another dimension, in which there is an active consciousness completely different from that of waking, and sensing stimuli occurs with totally unconscious "organs".

Theta waves reach a frequency reduction from 6 to 4 cycles per second, and the voltage rises up to 100 microvolts. Going further makes the brain reach the very deep sleep, without dreams, during which unconscious mind keeps main biological functions to the lowest level; electromagnetic waves (called "Delta") slow down to 0.5 -3 cycles per second, and the voltage rises up to 200 microvolts.

In this state knowledge becomes intuitive, conscious awareness is completely inhibited, the state of relaxation of body is complete, and insensitivity to external stimuli reaches its highest degree. For the purposes of this text it will be examined the Alpha state, to make some exercises useful to achieve, through use of effective techniques, best results in the sales process.

From level of wakefulness (Beta status) one can easily access Alpha state through common techniques of relaxation and mild hypnosis, to mitigate the "supervision" of the conscious mind and supersede its censorship. At the same time the unconscious mind is highlighted, therefore becoming particularly permeable and receptive to rewire the neural patterns of brain, which will lead to better sales performances.

A relaxation exercise to reach Alpha state

Put yourself in a reclined position, where you do not run the risk of being disturbed; the environment has to foster silence. A couch, a bed, the floor, are all suitable. A pillow under your head will be perfect, if you simply lie on the floor (so that the spine can relax even in the terminal area), arms have to be extended along the body, and legs stretched out, avoiding crossing.

As soon as the ideal position is reached, close your eyes and do some deep breaths, in order to oxygenate all brain cells, preparing them for the task. That done, stand still for a moment, feeling a sense of peace and comfort. At this point the protocol of deep relaxation begins.

You should go through each muscle group, focusing your attention on releasing all tensions behind specific order (better mental then verbal).

"Muscles of the skull, relaxed and abandoned; facial muscles relaxed and abandoned, neck muscles relaxed and abandoned." Continue like this until you mentioned all the muscle groups of the body.

At the same time it is useful to observe, with mind's eye, the muscles going from a state of tension to a state of absolute lack of tone. At the end, the heart and respiratory rates should have decreased, and brain waves should have approached the Alpha state. At this point, to further deepen the state of relaxation, mentally count up to ten, with slowness. At the end of the relaxation process, probably the state of abandonment is appropriate to allow the frequency of the electromagnetic waves of brain to go down until Alpha rhythm. This state is also naturally achieved the evening before going to sleep and in the morning, during the wake.

The Alpha state is the most propitious time to make affirmations and visualizations. One must remain in this state, in which it is only weakly receptive to stimuli coming from outside, for the time necessary to affirm and / or visualize. After that, you can slowly return to the waking state, giving tone to the muscles and opening your eyes.

Affirmations

Affirmations, since long time, are recognized as a powerful transformation tool. They function as a real programming language, which is able to rewire unconscious mind. Through specific methods that we will see later, the repetition of a message (verbal, mental, written) helps create new neural pathways in mind, which in turn change people's behavior. Affirmation is created and processed in conscious part of mind and then, through repetition, pervades unconscious side. Here thoughts of the individual can change at a deep level, change that is expressed in a new behavior, more productive of good results. There are several methods which can be used.

• By voice (the affirmation is repeated, preferably with a volume medium or medium-high;

• Written (write the affirmation, for 20 - 30 times, on a blank sheet). In this case the writing can be carried out in the state of normal wakefulness;

• Played through a voice player;

•Watched on a pc screen.

The unconscious mind is able, thanks to its incredible computing power (that famous 95%) to perform virtually any task. In fact, what each individual gets in a given moment of personal or professional life is a direct result of his actions, which in turn come from the decisions that the belief system takes. The chain is: belief, decision, action, result. Unconscious mind is unable to distinguish between reality and imagination and the individual, taking advantage of this, can deliberately rewire the neural pathways through affirmations.

Only entity able to provide instructions is the conscious mind that uses, as a faithful, tireless and effective servant the unconscious one. The role of the unconscious mind, as already seen, is not to judge, evaluate, correct, but only to follow all instructions it has received. These instructions lie in the core beliefs and deep thoughts. Affirmations are able to change them.

Affirmations need no confidence, from conscious mind, that they will work; just run the protocol with perseverance and tenacity, until the reprogramming is finished. Of course any belief against this technique risks to slow down the process, nevertheless without compromising it. You will realize the affirmation has taken deep roots (thus changing a core belief) from your thoughts and results you are able to obtain.

For example, if you want to improve your cold calling skills the relevant affirmation could be: "I, [name], am great in cold calling." You will realize affirmation took root when you experience less resistance to this activity, and indeed cold calling generates better results.

Affirmations are powerful tools to rewire the brain and transform results got in all life areas, but in this book we will explore this technique with particular reference to sales. To get the best possible result, affirmations must conform with the following rules.

- Present tense: affirmations are more effective when expressed in the present, because this is the time of action and results. Avoid future times, that would move to future also results.

- Affirmative: affirmations have to be affirmative; avoid negative forms, thus affirming what you want, instead of what you do not want. For example, avoid "I no longer want to lose customers" and replace it with "I am getting many new customers."

- Short and direct: if affirmations are short and direct are easier to pronounce, have a much better impact on unconscious mind, and are more clear. Being brief and direct adds power, because the underlying idea is clear and not disguised with unnecessary frills.

- Precise: you need to exactly verbalize what you want to achieve. Vague and imprecise affirmation leaves unconscious mind in the grip of doubts and uncertainty, lowering its effectiveness.

- Repetition: importance of repetition will never be overstated. Repeating affirmations settles more easily and more quickly into subconscious mind.

- Emotions: feeling desire and passion is a key ingredient of a good affirmation. It is necessary to be focused on meaning of the words, rather than repeat them like parrots.

- Tenacity: tenacity in repeating produces better results than a sporadic practice.

• Directly involve yourself: deeply customize affirmations, making it specific just for you. Begin it with "I, [name], ...". The stronger the feeling affirmation generates, the more profound the track it will save in mind, and the faster the time to achieve desired result.

• One at a time: especially in the early stages of use of this technique, it is recommended to begin to operate on just one area at a time. For example, if you believe you must get better in getting rapport, managing objections, and in customer needs' analysis, just begin with one of these three topics. As soon as you have got first results, you can tackle other areas. Just when you gain a complete experience of method, it is possible to work on several areas, in parallel, by rotate respective affirmations.

• Timing: apart from an artificially induced Alpha state, evening just before sleeping, and morning when you wake up, are two excellent moments for practicing affirmations. In these moments conscious awareness no longer (evening) or not yet (morning) has got complete control of mind, so affirmations work better, and more easily sediment down to unconscious. You might also plan other daily sessions, preferably during Alpha state.

Speed with which you'll experience first results is related with number of sessions carried out, keeping in mind that, at the beginning, affirmations manifest a certain degree of hysteresis to provide tangible results, even in case of frequent daily sessions. Anyway, plan 20 to 30 repetitions each session. It is better starting with simple goals, as any belief against such an approach could slow down the process. By achieving these initial simple goals you'll gain confidence, and therefore you will be able to aim high, and get results more quickly.

In all ways, it is quite common and frequent having doubts or feeling resistance affirming something that, following conscious mind's rules, is not actually already happened. Beginning to use this technique, affirming that something in your life / job is real, conscious mind can present a number of reasons why it does not believe what affirmations say. For example, imagine a salesman who wants to improve handling objections, and decides to affirm: "I, Joe, am very effective in dealing with objections." Conscious mind can then give birth to thoughts like, "Do not be stupid, when the customer objects you start quarrelling", or "The truth is that every objection makes you smaller and smaller." If, since the beginning, individual consciously had believed an affirmation was true, it would mean that he already holds relevant belief, and had already received corresponding benefits. So, in such a case, no need to affirm anymore! Truth is affirmations, almost always, trigger doubts from the conscious mind.

Doubts should be left free to pop up, as it is a process of "sanitizing" old fears. At the same time, avoid the desire to assess whether the affirmations are actually working or not, and continue practice. Confidence in this technique will rise when you will reap first successes. To address eventual strong resistances, use a sheet of paper divided into two columns. On the left you write the affirmation, on the right all contrary thoughts that arise.

Any resistance (apparently dictated by a logical and sequential way of thinking) that tends to cast doubts on affirmation, is symptom of a deep-seated belief that is contrary to what you are affirming. You should observe what are more frequently occurring doubts, e.g. "I do not deserve this kind of success", and addressing them with proper affirmation. Following the above example, an adequate affirmation could be: " I, Joe, deserve highest success in selling". If so, practicing it will make you experience the sabotaging belief slowly slip away.

When an affirmation takes root (starting to change your behavior and producing first results), usually first signs of acceptance arise, along with positive thoughts about the statement itself. This is the best signal that affirmation actually works. Response times are variable, and sometimes first positive results come after weeks and weeks of practice. This is due to the fact that old self-sabotaging beliefs and behaviors have probably been in place for a long time.

In these cases enthusiasm, discipline and persistence are needed, to ensure that affirmation settles properly. Neither helps being too impatient, constantly analyzing obtained results, and comparing them with those of the past, in a frantic attempt for a positive signal indicating proper functioning of the technique

Otherwise you would be like a farmer who, after having planted the seeds of a certain cultivar, continually unearth the seeds to check for new roots. He should better rely on the forces of nature, patiently waiting to see first leaves popping up from the ground.

Method, patience, awareness of the physiologically necessary time, enthusiasm, confidence and tenacity are qualities which open the way for brain rewiring through affirmations, without stifling the new positive trends that began to operate, albeit imperceptibly at first, and create best conditions for growing results.

In the world of sales, affirmations useful to trigger increases in performance are among the most varied and subjective, since they are directly linked to the specific needs of each salesman. On the other hand, sale is a complex phenomenon and is made by a series of steps deeply interconnected, which influence each other. In addition, affirmations should be surgically designed, so as to allow it to precisely act where there is a limiting belief at work. For these reasons, design of specific affirmation is entirely left to the reader. This book simply provides some examples, suitable for an even complete redesign.

- I, ..., get successful and increasing sales day in and day out

- I, ..., effectively manage the relationship with my clients

- I, ..., increase my influencing skills every day

- I, ..., handle objections with great effectiveness

- I, ..., every day I learn more and more from my sales activity

- I, ..., get more and more commissions day after day

Visualizations

As already seen, human brain treats vividly imagined facts almost the same way as real ones, setting in motion a series of physiological responses close to those of real situations.

I'm sure everyone can vividly remember   highly emotional moments occurred in the past, experiencing changes in the heart rate, breathing rate, muscles tension, just like going through the real experience once again.

Visualize, in practice, is to imagine as vividly as possible, a certain event (for example, for a salesman, a winning negotiation) using as many senses as possible. This technique provides the best results if practiced under a mild self-hypnosis, like the Alpha state.

Use hear (listen the words of your buyer), touch (feel at your fingertips the smoothness of the folder used for the presentation), view (see the scene in great details,; smell (feel the typical smell of the factory / office of that particular customer). All that complemented by feelings of joy, professionalism and personal power, the same feelings you experienced at that time.

Unconscious mind considers a so vividly imagined fact as a real one, and treats it as a program string, saving it in its deep parts, and finally making it available whenever you will have to negotiate again.

This technique indicates the unconscious mind the direction you want to follow and goals you want to achieve. Unconscious mind, so well briefed, becomes a kind of autopilot that guides you where it has understood you want to go.

Since decades ago, visualization techniques are used in many sport fields, where is part of usual training of many olympic athletes. As an example, I quote a study made by an experienced group of Soviet scientists, on a team of highly skilled athletes, ahead of the 1980 Olympics in Lake Placid.

The team was splitted into four groups: the first group made 100% physical training; the second made 75% of physical training and 25% of mental training; the third made 50% of physical training and 50% of mental training; the fourth group made 25% of physical training and 75% of mental training.

The results were astonishing: during preparations for olympic games, the fourth group got better results than the third, which in turn did better than the second; the less significant performances came from the first group.

Dr. Charles Garfield, a NASA researcher, who had the chance to check those results, said: "When visualizing, these athletes create a mental image of each precise movement they would perform, rehearsing it many times with their mind's eyes. This creates a number of neural paths in their gray matter, able to facilitate a lot the live sport action."

As well as affirmations, visualizations must also be made in the present tense. This means that you must live, through the mind's eye, the exact scene as it would happen in reality, in the present moment. Otherwise, viewing the same scene as it will occur in the future, means investing in the desire; in such a case, the result will not be as effective. This technique is well known to people who are used to make meditation sessions. Obviously, first visualizations won't be that easy: thought shifts, distractions, some fatigue usually are something easy to be experienced. Practicing will make everything easier.

If hurdles persist, you might want to use a technique called streaming. In practice this is to make a verbal description of the scene you are visualizing, in as much detail as possible. Describing the scene in detail helps to focus on it, and images gradually become more vivid and more durable.

As mentioned, it is important to "incorporate" as many senses as possible in this mental experience, including emotional content that might exists and that you would feel if the experience was real. That may sound complex, however isn't more complicated than mimicking the activities of any actor. Actors, in fact, read a script, identify themselves into their role, and keep emotions and behaviors of their character.

Anchors

You have certainly experienced (maybe more than once) listening to a song, and going back in past times, reliving past situations in great detail. In practice, the song has had the role of a sort of trigger, making you feeling certain emotions. The same effect might come from a perfume, a place, a movie, a person, some words, and so on.

All these elements (music, scent, place, words, ...) are called anchors, just because they anchor a stimulus (auditory, olfactory, visual, kinesthetic) to certain emotions and feelings. In practice, as soon as you hear (or see, touch, feel) the stimulus the feelings / emotions that originally you experienced are felt again.

For example, imagine that a certain night a person has found his soul mate, while he was in a disco; "I Feel Love" by Donna Summers was playing. Of course, that situation was charged by intense emotions (pleasure, happiness, love, ...) As a result, it is likely that this person, whenever he listens the same track, almost entirely relive all the emotions felt during that event.

All that opens great possibilities to individuals and, of course, also to sales people. As an example, let's say you have to make a difficult sales call, and would like to be at your best (in terms of energy, enthusiasm, physiological state, ...) in order to successfully close the deal. What about finding a switch that can instantly puts you in that exact mood?

This switch exists, and is an anchor. In practice, you can anchor your best and productive mood to a certain stimulus; when you need to enter in that mood, just push the switch (in jargon I say "launch the anchor") and instantly you enter into the desired way. It seems an useful tool, doesn't it?

For being effective an anchor must be installed following certain rules:

• The stimulus (in the above case the track) must be unique

• The stimulus must act in the very moment when the person is experiencing the emotion at its highest intensity; in other words, the emotion felt has to reach its peak when the stimulus is heard (seen, touched,...)

• The stimulus must be repeated many times, to permanently install the anchor.

In practice, it is sufficient to anchor to a given stimulus (a gesture, a word) the mood you want to access to. The launch of the stimulus (the anchor) allow instant access to the anchored state (the mood you want to access to) facilitating the achievement of success.

Assume that you want to anchor a feeling of great confidence in your sales skills. The protocol is as follows.

1. Sit in a comfortable chair, relax for a few moments, regulate breathing; decide which will be the stimulus to use (let's call it the anchor, and it will be firmly clenching the right fist);

2. Recall to your mind a time that you felt yourself full of energy and great success, perfectly adequate, and full of confidence in your sales skills; recall to your mind how did you feel, what emotions did you experience, the rhythm of your breath, your posture;

3. Strengthen all that emotions, and let them grow as much as possible;

4. Now that you feel they have grown, double their intensity, then double them again and again (feel free to jump, pirouette, scream, if it helps you);

5. When all that reaches its peak, clench the right fist;

7. After a couple seconds, relax, breath deeply, and repeat the protocol for 5-10 times (the fist must be clenched, every time, with exactly the same force and in the exact same fashion);

8. Finally, if the anchor is installed properly, simply clenching the left fist (so doing, you "launch the anchor") to access the state of mind that you have anchored.

The anchor can be anything: a song, a gesture, a word, a movement (of course is better if it is something easily made in public …). When you face the need to access to the anchored mood, just throw the anchor and, instantly, you will get the desired mood!

9 – CONCLUSIONS

Brain potential of each individual is huge, much bigger than what is deemed possible. The limits of what people are able to achieve are far beyond what is normally believed.

The point is that far the largest portion of this potential deeply lies within the depths of the unconscious mind, an area normally not accessible by the volition. So, as a general rule, people are used to harness just a small fraction of that potential, thus making difficult reaching top performance in private life, as well as in professional one.

If we would be used to tap into a larger slide of that potential, life could become much easier, and also very ambitious goals might be hitted with ease. Think how wonderful life could be, if everybody could get better in harnessing also their deep resources!

This also applies to sales, in which beliefs, self-esteem and body language are almost always decisive to achieve excellence. However, every salesman is able to remove the blocks that prevent him from flying as high as he deserves. The techniques showed in this book come from the latest schools of thought regarding how our mind operates, and if applied with enthusiasm, energy, resilience and determination are able to change any sales result, forever. So, read them, learn them, apply them, and let them lead you to reach what you truly want for your sales career, forever!